LOVE AND LIFE

LOVE AND LIFE

by Leo Jung

1892— 1987

PHILOSOPHICAL LIBRARY
NEW YORK

Copyright, 1979, by Philosophical Library, Inc.
15 East 40 Street, New York, N. Y. 10016
All rights reserved.

Library of Congress Catalog Card No. 79-87873
SBN 8022-2355-9

Manufactured in the United States of America

Dedicated to the memory of the sainted
SAMUEL ROSEN
—an ideal husband and father, communal
leader and generous trustee of Congregation
Kehillat Jeshurun, Yeshiva University,
Beth Israel Hospital, and munificent
contributor to Federation of Jewish
Philanthropies and the United Jewish Appeal.

CONTENTS

Guidelines to a Happy Marriage   1

The Problems of Our Women in Our Own Times   19

Woman's Three-Fold Role   31

Knowledge and Love in Rabbinic Lore   35

Man's Knowledge of God   39

Of Love and Knowledge   53

PREFACE

In one of my early books, "Crumbs and Character," I quote the Talmud's statement: "The moral power of a nation is exhibited in its attitude towards woman." That attitude, in the mind of too many Jews, is the best kept secret of their philosophy of life. That ignorance has been the source of much confusion and more violation of the Torah's laws and principles. All sorts of queer substitutes and cults have benefitted from the well-nigh universal unawareness of precious guidance. The simple prose of this slender volume is meant to supply basic information for the renaissance of our folk's supreme asset: the Jewish home.

Leo Jung

GUIDELINES TO A HAPPY MARRIAGE

This work is not meant for people who allow themselves to be governed by their impulses rather than by the moral tradition of our people, who interpret love in terms of sexual enterprise rather than mutual and consistent awareness of human dignity and dedication. Their common excuse—"everybody does it"—is as unwise as it is unworthy. In that respect, Jews have been taught to respect love and stay ever conscious of responsibility for the abiding happiness of the life-mate. They must not be "like everybody else," co-religionists or outsiders. Such people need prolonged, special personal attention rather than the perusal of essays, short or long. I would not want to exclude any one, however, from my interest or attention. It is a social and personal duty to point out to them that the reduction of love to sex robs them of the abiding sense of belonging, of mutual dedication for life. Such dedication will prevent resentment, which, of late, has been leading to a calamitous number of divorces.

The oldest document in human history providing for the protection of the bride is the *Ketubah* (the Hebrew Marriage Document). In the presence of two witnesses, the groom hands it to her. It contains this declaration:

1

"Become thou my wife according to the Law of Moses and Israel and I shall serve you, honor you, and provide for you according to the tradition of Jewish husbands who serve, honor, and provide for their wives in sincerity."

I

In many a case, there is no relationship between knowledge of *The Shulhan Arukh** and an awareness of what love between husband and wife must mean.

In family affairs, personal and moral responsibility about one's mate and his or her needs crowns the ritual of the law involved. The woman as a person must be consistently considered.

I remember a precious young woman, whose marital problems I endeavored to solve, telling me: "After every intercourse, I cried bitterly."

I know of a young rabbi, scholar, gentleman, whose parents and friends had so little prepared him for the actuality of the first consummation that it ended in embarrassed confusion. He had to go to a physician for advice about how to proceed. Young people may need, beyond the rabbi's attention, psychiatric counselling, offered by one who deeply understands Jewish law and love.

Happy marriage is a stage of development when the two partners have grown to think of each other's happiness and have left behind the concentration on their own narcissistic gratification.

The wife must be as sensitive to her husband's feeling, personal, emotional and sexual problems as he must stay aware of hers.

*The authoritative, ever unfinished Code of Jewish Law, developing by application of principle and precedent to new conditions.

2

If a husband is a realist and the wife an optimist, or vice versa, their loving discussion will not only achieve abiding peace, but, in the process will enrich and develop both personalities. All problems—troubling their loving peace, involving doubt or difficulty—should find a solution before the couple retires to sleep or else disagreements may become unpleasant tensions.

II

The Talmud[1] refers to the problem through a rather odd story. An innocent would-be-*hatan* (fiancé), deprived of any parental or friendly guidance and frightened about a possibly wrong approach, chose a curious way to obtain the required knowledge. He crawled under the bed, listening to his master's approach to his wife.

The disciple's youthful impulsiveness evoked his teacher's reproof. The student was correct in stating (*Torah he velilmod ani tzarikh*) that our sacred texts offered direction and guidance in every aspect of life which he was seeking. The teacher's sharp rebuke indicated that the youth should have asked him for detailed direction instead of tasteless intrusion into his home.

It is an essential duty of parents to convey that information, or, if they feel themselves incapable or unwilling, to ask a physician or a well-aware Rav to provide that guidance.

It would be advantageous to make available to couples contemplating marriage sexual counseling before marriage as well as after—under the auspices of the rabbinate, consideration of personal, religious, as well as sexual aspects of one's relationship with the marital partner.

During the forty-four years that I taught at Yeshiva

University, I warned my students (many of whom were candidates for the rabbinate) never to officiate at a wedding without having had a conference with the young couple (of at least an hour or two duration) weeks in advance of the actual ceremony. That conference ought to be based not only on loyalty to Jewish Law but also on awareness, reverence and appreciation of the spiritual elements of physical love.

The couple should discuss with the rabbi in the early period of their engagement—rather than at the eleventh hour—the responsibilities and opportunities of marriage. The rabbi could then decide whether they require further discussion with him or other professional assistance.

For the husband, awareness of, and respect for, the wife's intellectual, emotional and physical needs is essential. It promotes and sustains marital happiness.

"About a man who loves his wife as himself, who honours her more than himself, Scripture states:

'And thou shalt know that thy tent is in peace.'"[2]

Whatever problems arise during the marriage should be discussed openly and fully between the two partners. *They must share their thoughts with each other.* That will prevent small grievances or annoyances from festering and assuming major proportions.

Never go to sleep angry with your spouse! It is better to discuss the problems openly and fully than to let them fester and magnify—because of persistent silence.

Before the wedding ceremony, the Rabbi should again seek occasion for a private *siha* (conversation) with the young man and tell him: "When you are alone together, first talk to her about the joy of the occasion, her beauty, her sweetness, then kiss her and hold her tight and continue the same affectionate confabulation. Hold her tight

4

but do not approach her until you know intuitively that her inner trembling has stopped."[3]

Many young women are afraid not only of the pain involved, but of being possessed. And every truly loving, wise husband must not for a moment, forget that feeling, nor may the truly loving wife ignore his impulsive longing and embarrassment.[4]

The marital relationship involves capacity for patience, understanding and empathy—total dedication.

III

The loving act, whilst occasionally shocking to the young woman, renders her husband completely exhausted. Yet, it is most important that before the actual physical separation, he spend some time speaking tenderly with her.

I cannot forget the confidence of another young woman who said to me: "At the end of the first night, I felt that I was only a means to an end."

IV

A sensitive young husband, especially in the earliest stages of marriage, will call his wife at least once a day. He will bring her —at least once a week—some symbol of his attachment: a book, a box of candy, some flowers. During the twelve days of *Niddah*,* many a woman feels utterly alone and a good husband will accordingly call her several times every day during the *Niddah* period, and should

*Period of menstruation and physical separation for seven days following the five days of the menses.

bring her several such gifts to make her feel she is in his mind and heart, no matter how busy he may be in his business or profession.

He should never forget to bring her a bunch of flowers on Friday afternoon. It will make a world of difference to their *Shabbat Menuhah* (Sabbath rest) and *Shalom Bayit* (peace of home).

However, more than any other gift, is the gift of one's self. As Emerson put it:

"Things are not gifts, only apologies for gifts, the greatest gift is a portion of one's self."

Abiding communication between the couple sharing every-thing—success, disappointments and even the nitty gritty of the routine of daily life. (Professor Jerry Hochbaum's precious statement.)

The twelve days of complete physical separation between husband and wife prevent married relations from becoming a cheap, drab routine affair.

The monthly *Tevilah* (immersion) in the *Mikvah* (the ritual bath) prepares a new honeymoon without any ugly experience or feeling that married relations have become purely physical.

V

Modern life is very exacting.

The husband may be very busy, annoyed, disappointed at the end of his working period. But when he comes home, the joy of meeting his beloved one must bring him a psalm in his heart and a smile on his lips. For he is not returning merely to his apartment but to his comrade, his life's mate. The wife, too, may be returning home from a

6

day's work, burdened by her own difficulties and frustrations. *Sharing thoughts on all problems minimizes them.*

Undoubtedly, problems occur—not only between husband and wife, but between employers and employees, colleagues, friends, and strangers. They should not appear on the face of the lover (wife or husband) returning home. Unless special circumstances demand immediate discussion, it is after dinner, when they sit hand in hand, that they should lovingly, wisely, and quietly discuss both the problems and annoyances and the way to prevent and overcome them.

Impatience, hatred, and meanness are apparently unavoidable in many outside relations. In the *Mikdash Me'at* (The little Sanctuary) of the home, they may be discussed as some of the dust of the earth within the atmosphere of total dedication to each other's happiness.

In Jewish law a woman does not, by the marriage document, surrender control of her body.[5] To illustrate what I have in mind, please remember this: whilst cohabitation with a woman under a certain age is considered rape in American law, and may result in many years of prison or penitentiary to the man, it is taken for granted that once one has married a woman, she surrenders control of her body. Hence those abominable ads in the newspapers: "My wife having left my bed and board, I will not be responsible for her debts."

Completely different is the Jewish attitude. There, consent is essential in marriage. On the one hand, Judaism does not look down upon physical love.[6] We are composed of body and soul, and it is natural, human, and legitimate that love expresses itself in both forms. On the other hand, Judaism teaches that physical love is justified only where back of it is not only affection, but respect for the partner and consideration for her and his abiding happiness.[7]

7

According to Jewish law, it is morally and ritually a very grave offense for the husband to approach his wife carnally without her consent.

A few months ago, there sat opposite me in my study a young man, very much favored by nature and circumstances: handsome, educated, charming and wealthy. He was speaking glowingly of his fiancée, and he said: "I am madly in love. I love her more than ever any man could have loved a woman." I listened to him for some time, and finally I said: "I don't believe what you are saying." He flared up. "Do you doubt my veracity, Sir?" My answer was: "I don't doubt your veracity, but I doubt your ability to see the truth. You have been sitting here for almost half an hour, talking about the joy of marriage, about her beauty and charm, but not a single word has escaped you that indicated any real sense of responsibility. You took it for granted that you would be very happy, but you did not indicate in any manner that you were deeply interested in anyone's happiness but your own. What you really meant when you said 'I am madly in love with her' was 'she is beautiful, and it will be wonderful to kiss her and caress her.' But you had never begun to think about your obligation to establish and maintain her serenity."

According to Jewish law, a husband must never take his wife for granted. He must obtain her consent even in marriage. He must never approach her without her agreement. Physical love is the normal crowning of unity of heart and mind, but a wife, Jewishly speaking, should never become a means to the husband's ends. This applies at all times, so that the Jewish woman should be able to look herself square in the face ten or twenty years after marriage, and feel that marriage has brought her comradeship, understanding, intimate friendship, but that her girlhood dreams had also become true, that there is nothing to be ashamed of, nothing to regret in her new relations. It implies at all times this assurance of her personal dignity and self-respect.

The principle of consent applies with double force during the period of her menstruation and for certain days thereafter. This is the famous Jewish twelve-days law, concerning which Mary Stopes, one of the world's leading authorities on marriage relations, says that it is the only system of life and law that protects the physical and spiritual welfare of young women.

There is one great danger to marriage: that marital relations become a routine affair, like eating and drinking. Too often marriage starts with excess and ends with surfeit. The new experience is very enchanting to the young husband, and, beset by overwhelming emotion, he may make demands on his wife that would cause her to set aside the paramount asset of her freedom, never to regain it. More than one bark of marriage has foundered on the cliffs of uncontrolled desire. What we call Jewish marriage law is essentially a combination of principles and practices devised to protect woman's freedom. Authorities know today that for a week after her period, woman is not at her peak. The menses often cause a nervousness and irritation which do not disappear before a week. The Torah is most anxious to protect woman during that period. It is essential for husband and wife to realize that marriage is more than physical love. It implies not only consideration, patience and affection, but infinite trust and perpetual, boundless comradeship. During these twelve days when there is no physical approach, husband and wife become conscious of these other facets of married happiness. They recognize that sex is neither nothing nor everything. It is a powerful factor in marriage relations, but there are other drives and sentiments that may greatly affect the happiness of the partners. During these twelve days, husband and wife learn to be exceedingly considerate of each other, and that attitude then projects itself upon the end of the separation when the love cycle is taken up again. There is no staleness, no excess, no surfeit, but a restrained happy anticipation of complete love when husband and wife are both at ease: emotionally, physically and spiritually.

This is how Jewish law protects the freedom of woman. It proclaims the duty to interrupt the love cycle when the menses are expected. It enjoins that it may not be taken up before the bath of immersion has been taken. And this bath of immersion is not legitimate before twelve days. Thus the twelve days of freedom through separation are guaranteed to the woman, become self-evident to the man and raise the level and the tone of their married life.

Undoubtedly you have heard of the reactions to this law of immersion. Some of your friends have condemned it, others have sneered at it. That attitude is due partly to ignorance of the motive of this law as revealed in Jewish literature, and partly, perchance, to the defective background of the objector's youth. The familiar argument is that the purpose of the *mikvah* is merely cleanliness, that in antiquity there were no opportunities for bathing, and that modern plumbing takes such excellent care of these needs as to render the *mikvah* unnecessary. The same type of argument is used against the dietary laws and is based on the same type of ignorance. The Torah does nowhere state that the motive of the dietary laws is hygienic. In the classic passage of Leviticus, the purpose expressly stated is that of promoting God-consciousness or holiness. Undoubtedly, as divine laws, they are beneficial also from a hygienic and biological point of view. But their purpose in both cases is moral and spiritual.

When the *Mishnah*, including the law of *mikvah*, was put together, we lived under the rule of the Romans, and one of the seven wonders was their sumptuous baths, the very ruins of which excite the admiration of experts because of their luxuriousness and of their ingenious hygienic devices. With all its glory, modern plumbing could not improve on that. That will dispose of the plumbing argument. But the purpose of the Jewish laws of family purity, as indicated before, is purely spiritual. They have to do not merely with cleanliness but with purity, with the right mutual attitude of the two partners, with the freedom and self-respect of the wife, with the high level of the family atmosphere. Pragmatically, these laws have proved themselves productive of fine spirit, abiding serenity, and such ethical power in the Jewish family as have enabled it to weather all the storms of history, and survive Roman persecution, medieval cruelty, and all the horrors of the ghetto. Where in modern home this rite is observed, it helps to bring about equally fine results.

Whence then developed the mocking attitude toward that sacred institution? To my mind, undoubtedly, it stemmed from the well-nigh criminal negligence of earlier generations of Orthodox Jews in this country who built these sanctuaries of family purity in undesirable locations and permitted them to deteriorate by neglect. Jewish fathers and husbands were so indifferent to the aesthetic sensibilities of their daughters and wives as to impose upon them visits to these *mikvaoth* which would cause revulsion and associate this holy law with an atmosphere of squalor. I remember a number of such loathsome places both in the Middle West and in New York City and I cannot criticize too sharply the carelessness which made such conditions possible. Coupled with the unwillingness or inability of the rabbis to discuss this all-important subject and with a lack of informed rebellion among women (who should have refused to get married before the community established decent *mikvaoth*), the situation prevailed which rendered such hostility on the part of the half-informed and uninformed young women more than intelligible.

11

Judaism recommends early marriage. The passage in *Pirke Avoth* "At eighteen to the marriage canopy" need, of course, not be taken literally. It surely is not a command, for the same paragraph speaks of "forty for the acquisition of wisdom," and that surely is neither a command nor expressive of general experience. It is rather to be taken as a contemporary version of an abiding principle. Early marriage has been recommended as the Jewish solution of a problem that impinges on questions of mental, emotional, physical, and economic maturity.

As major objections to early marriage the following may be cited: the young people very often are emotionally unstable; they choose very often out of an impulse, because of one particular factor that proves irresistible, such as beautiful face or figure, intellectual brilliance, or financial assets.

The young people do not know that a successful marriage must be based on an all around fitness of the partners, that boy and girl must have many basic matters in common. Swept off their feet by the attraction of one or two points, the young people regret soon and help swell the number of divorces. American colleges of late have instituted marriage courses to promote a general awareness of the problems and of the needs for planning. Clergymen of all denominations should consider it a moral obligation to either encourage attendance at these courses or to offer some such guidance themselves. Considerable reading and experience will be necessary for such guidance to be fruitful, encouraging, and pleasant.

Early marriage is considered "impossible" because of the groom's financial insufficiency. The economic problem should be tackled boldly. Jewish daughters ought to be taught to demand a minimum of financial comfort for the early years of their married life. They should be willing to enlarge the margin of luxury as the husband develops his economic prowess or his professional ability. Otherwise they force this cruel dilemma upon the young man: From the age of twenty to twenty-five sublimate his creative urges by writing a thesis, by building a movement, or a business. At that age he should have found his mate, and married her. By then they both may be presumed to understand that the major benefit of marriage lies in the devotion, the affection, the friendship it implies, in what the partners are, and not in what they have. Parents can cooperate in this task by changing their attitude towards their own possessions. To leave money to the children at father's death means to provide them with affluence at a time when they are at the peak of their own economic power and where this extra possession is not of crucial importance. Rather should parents who have means offer some of it to their children as a gift or a loan for the first five years of their married life, in order to bridge the difference between the incipient earning power and the actual requirements of a simple life. In this manner the father's possessions will be of profound significance to the children. Otherwise the youth of twenty-five, handicapped by comparative poverty, will hesitate to contract marriage, and either remain continent, and by denying the claims of nature become liable to some sort of psychic disturbance, or will choose the cheaper way of prenuptial adventures and endanger, if not the health of the wife and unborn child, surely the level of his married life.

But the community too, has a part to play in the solution of this problem. Not all young people have been "wise in the selection of their parents." Some will be unable to provide them in the first years of their married lives with the differential between what they earn and what they need. Again, because of this, many men wait too long before they offer their hand and heart to a young woman; the result is a misalliance between an elderly bachelor and a young girl which too often spells broken homes. The children of such homes in too many cases are found in the waiting rooms of psychiatrists, before the judges in General Sessions, and in sanitariums for the mentally deranged.

In ancient Israel we had an institution that, in many Jewish communities, has persisted to our days. Its purpose was the dowering of poor brides. I submit as translation into modern life a community provision of a loan or a gift to young couples, that would enable them to seek fulfillment and stability at an earlier period, and would greatly diminish the hazards of marriage, would give children born to young parents a better chance of wholesome development, and reduce by millions the cost of providing for the neurotic population of the country.

VI

In the home, the atmosphere should be less of *Mitzvah* (commandment) than of *Simhah shel Mitzvah* (the joy of conforming to His Law) and our folk's way of life.

The root of the Hebrew word for *Hinnukh* (education) is *Hekh* (palate). Modern archaeology has taught us that when the Semitic tribes, as early as the time of Abraham, introduced the young boy into the cult of the tribe, the father used to smear his palate with honey, to render that occasion — both at the moment and in its memory — as sweet as possible.

Jewish education, to be successful, requires that tender, wise — even though firm — treatment, so does successful marriage.

There must be an agreement as to the roles as husband and wife, father and mother. Such consensus guarantees a successful marriage, combining the historical glory of the Jewish

14

home with the legitimate aspects of woman's liberation and its expression within and outside the home.[8]

Even if one mate does not agree with the other's approach, in front of the children they must present a united front and be loyal to each other's directives.

VII

The young couple must share thoughts and problems, relaxation, exercise, music and work. They must become ever more acquainted to convey to their adolescent children a sense of inner peace.

The Dietary Laws, the Shabbat, the *Tzedakkah Pushka* (charity box) — all convey, in their way, the aspects of Jewish social idealism which render comradeship delightful.

VIII

Most important is the attitude of in-laws toward the young couple. They should practice love from a distance, encourage the young couple to stand on their own feet, and above all avoid in-law troubles of constant interference, criticism, or surplus suggestions.

Once upon a time I received this lesson. A lovely young girl who had attended a lecture of mine at a New York college and whom I had agreed to see, burst into uncontrolled weeping because "My mother annoys my husband by criticizing what she calls his insufficient respect for me. She then plagues me, warning me to be careful about my self-respect. Her daily telephone calls are a genuine plague."

I succeeded in solving that problem by telling the

shocked mother-in-law that there are three bad words in the English language: "Communism — which destroys the nation; Fascism — which destroys the group; and in-laws — which destroy the family."

IX

Altogether it is important that the husband and wife need not be totally alike. They must, of course, agree on basic principles — such as devotion to Torah, folk and all humans, above all, consistent conduct of honesty and compassion.

They should agree to disagree agreeably on all matters which do not touch fundamentals.

They should share problems and, by their various approaches, each will promote and indeed ennoble the personality of the life's mate.

X

The married woman must always be conscious of the obligation to take care of her aesthetic needs. Greeting her husband in a not-quite-clean or somewhat torn or otherwise negligent attire, will make him unconsciously look down on her and, in worst cases, may render another woman, well-dressed, well-mannered, charming, anything from a temptation to a cause of disregard and disrespect for his wife.

The husband owes his wife the same respect in regard to cleanliness and neatness, and cultured behavior.

NOTES

1. Berakhot 62a
2. Yebamot 62b
   Job V, 24
3. Baba Batra 10b
4. Zohar Pinhas CCXXV
5. Jung, Leo. *Rhythm of Life*
   Jung, Moses. *Modern Marriage*
   Lamm, Norman. *Hedge of Roses*
   Hoenig, Sidney. *Jewish Family Life*
6. Erubin 100b
   Pessahim 49b
   Shulhan Arukh, Evan Ha-Ezer XXV s.v. piyyus
   The articles by Nima Adlerblum, Rivka R. Jung and Cecil Roth in Leo Jung's *Woman;* third volume of The Soncino Edition of The Jewish Library.
7. Silverman, Hirsch L. *Marital Counseling, Marital Therapy*
8. Stopes, Mary. *Wise Parenthood*

THE PROBLEMS OF OUR WOMEN IN OUR OWN TIMES

"Im en adam messim atzmo ka'midbar eino yakhol layda Torah u'mitzvot." (If a man does not consider himself as in the position of a wilderness, he will never understand the meaning of Torah and Mitzvot.) Ba'al Haturim, Bamidbar I.[1]

What represents a *midbar* (wilderness)? There are three kinds: the first is agricultural, as was encountered by our forefathers in Ancient Palestine; the second one is political and social, as suffered by His folk in the countless years of *galut;* the third is the desert of an individual's problems, often overwhelming and apparently hopeless.

I

In contemporary experience it is Israel which, through her *halutzim, mad'anim* (pioneers and scientists) has been changing its *midbar* (wilderness) to *Gan HaShem* (a garden of God). Their latest research has even made possible the use of algae as a source of oil. The back-breaking effort of the scholars of the Hebrew University has been supporting

19

the unique *bittahon* (trust, faith, feeling of security) of the countless halutzim who — in Arabic parlance — were *bot'him* (leaning against the immovable rock of our history): "*Ki beyah HaShem tzur olamim* (The Lord God, the Rock of the Ages)."[2]

The *midbar* of American Jewish youth shall be conquered by genuine patriotism which endorses every liberal movement. Of decisive significance is the phenomenon of science crowned by abiding, consistent, social consciousness.

In similar manner, against apparently insufferable handicaps, our people by their stiff-necked faith, have survived the bitter desert of inhumanity and helped to build up whatever culture and genuine civilization blesses the unhappy world of today.

II

For the *midbar* faced by every individual adolescent — and beyond that period — Judaism recommends not only philosophical faith in the wisdom of the omnipotent Lord, but in particular, contemplation and consideration of the family.

"*Ish al diglo be'otot lebet avotam* (Each person by the flag and standard of his family)"[3] to enable him to become a *hayyal* (soldier) *saviv le'ohel moed* (around the Tent of Meeting) which raised the hopeless milieu of the *midbar* to a congregational sanctuary full of optimism, a sense of responsibility and assurance of ultimate peace and happiness.

This is what the *Midrash Tanhumah* had in mind when it said: "*HaKaddosh Barukh Hu her'ah ahavato keshetzivah le'Mosheh Rabbenu la'assot degalim ve'otot* (The Lord manifested His love for Israel as he bade our teacher Moshe to make flags and standards for his flock)."[4]

We live in a permissive period today, and many people are under the impression that this is because we have burst out of an age-old strait-jacket. But the fact is that societies swing between prudery and permissiveness; this certainly occurred in Rome, which passed from strictness to license between the time of the Antonines and the Emperors, while the converse change took place in England when Christian missionaries and the Norman invaders between them clamped down on the fertility worship and pagan jollity (largely Celtic in origin) which they found there.

Since such swings have occurred so often in the past, we can be sure that they will occur again, so we must take seriously the possibility that our current permissiveness will again be replaced by severity, perhaps within the life-span of our own grandchildren. Indeed, there are already some signs of a swing-back.

III

In Search of the Holy Land

To be fit for a successful search for the Holy Land, one must be "every inch a prince (*kol nassi bahem*)."[5] Because ten of the spies who undertook to go there were merely *elected* instead of the *élite,* they failed and brought back an evil report which inflicted upon their people forty years in the wilderness before their eventual approach to the Jordan River. The classical *halutzim*, upon whom the fate of every Jewish generation in every century rests, are men of vision, determination, courage to face great obstacles, but above all, representing nobility of character.

21

How can we achieve vital identification of our burdened, troubled, rebellious, precious youth, identification with Judaism and Israel?

On another occasion, I've suggested the addition of one word to our list of confessions uttered on Yom Kippur. The list begins: "*Ashamnu* — we are guilty, *Bagadnu* — we have been faithless . . ." My addition would read: *Hiznahnu* — we have neglected." That applies in particular to parents and community of the Jewish boy of today and in particular of the Jewish girl of today.

We used to feel rather at ease about their Jewish future because their home offered the most excellent laboratory for training in the wisdom and nobility of our faith. Back of our optimism was the thought of the mother as the priestess of the home, whose mind, time and energy was dedicated to the development — in her beloved little ones — of incipient joy, pride, and loyalty. Times have changed. Many a wife accompanies her husband to business from nine in the morning to six in the evening. Many others follow professions of their own, demanding similar time and concentrated effort. Only a small minority of our children, especially of our girls, receive the benefits of Day Schools which, in turn, if they lead from nursery to college — but not otherwise — promise educational and spiritual success. We must do our duty to our girls in particular.

All that follows is in complete accord with the *Din Torah* — the time-hallowed application, not adaptation, of Torah-true precedent and principle to new conditions.

The occasional over-emphasis notwithstanding, the woman's lib movement has its strong points. Jewish religious and educational movements from the Women's Branch of the Union of Orthodox Jewish Congregations to Torah and Massorah, from Woman's Mizrahi to Hadassah, indicate a much appreciated and successful endeavor of our women in the second half of the twentieth century.

Important, too, is the new program of the housewife who, beyond her domestic role, has flourished in business, professional and social work, which represents a very valid new asset of our folk in the Golah as well as in Israel.

To offer them respectful, loving recognition and consistent encouragement will spell both wisdom and justice.

A luminous example may be offered by the interpretation which a contemporary Gaon gave to the young wife's right to bestow the name of *her* relative upon the firstborn child. The saintly scholar said: "Often the young mother feels she is cut off from her family: only the husband's parents and relatives are the major influences in the new home. To counteract that depressing feeling, the privilege of naming the firstborn was bestowed not upon the father but upon the mother."[6]

IV

I think that you read The Sunday Times, The Cleveland Plain Dealer, The Chicago Tribune and other Sunday newspapers and that you are as hurt as I am when I read that Mr. or Miss Goldstein was married by a Monsignor, that Mr. or Miss Goldberg was married by a Lutheran Pastor or that Mr. or Miss Cohen was married by a Justice of the Peace.

We ask ourselves why does this happen to our fold? Judaism is very much in advance of other religious and governmental laws as they touch upon woman's position, dignity, and care. The first document in human history showing positive and abiding interest in womanhood is the *Ketubah* in which the would-be husband declares: "*Hevi li le'intu kedat Mosheh veYissrael ve'ana eflah, okir, ve'afarness yatikhi likhi bekushta* (Become thou my wife according to the

23.

law of Moses and Israel and I shall serve you, honour you, and provide for you in sincerity)."[7]

The laws of *Taharat Ha'mishpahah* (Family Purity)[7a] are fundamentally meant to protect the couple, inspired by woman's dignity, self-respect and by a mutual sense of belonging in the hearts of both mates.

The *Tur Even Ha'ezer* (the code on which the Shulhan Arukh is built) quotes the law that a husband is not permitted to leave the house for commercial or any other purpose without his wife's permission, and, even if she gives him that permission, it is not proper for him to stay away for more than a month.

Reb Moshe Alshekh, in his responsum says: "A man must not leave his wife without her express permission to travel far away, even *letzorekh mitzvah* (for religious purpose) or *letzorekh parnassah* (for economic reasons). How much less would he be permitted to leave for the sake of a mere trip!

Rambam, in *Sefer ha'Mitzvot*[8] decides: "Even if it be a trip to the Holy Land, with the exception of visits to the Holy Places and the graves of *Tzadikkim* (pious sages), which may be considered exceptional *Mitzvot*."

With all that, definitely a glorious asset of our faith, why are so many of our sons and daughters not afraid to leave our tradition and engage in intermarriage?

At Harvard, a few years ago, a student — after my lecture — asked: "Rabbi, how can we in 1968 go by a Code of Laws printed in 1552?" I told him that the *Shulhan Arukh* is the authoritative but ever unfinished Code of Jewish Law. From the first Code — the *Mishnah* — through the *Talmud*, the *Rishonim* (Sages before the sixteenth century) and the *Aharonim* (Scholars afterwards), there are countless discussions and applications of precedents and principles to changing conditions, without interfering with — but, indeed, in full accord with — the authority of The Oral Law.

Rabbi Yohanan ben Zakai abolished the bitter waters of the woman suspected of adultery because the men of his generation had ceased to be inspiring examples of marital fidelity.

Jewish Law does not allow the giving or taking of interest on loans from a fellow Jew. Modern business conditions, however, require a great deal of credit. To overcome that difficulty, the *Hetter Iska*[9] was introduced: permission of an investment in which the lender and the borrower share loss and profit and, according to which — if the borrower engages in work — he must be paid for it, lest his labor spell an interest.

After the Second World War, Rabbi Kahane, Chief Rabbi of Warsaw, headed a group of scholars who dealt with the dreadful problem of countless *agunot* (women whose husbands had disappeared), victims of Nazi and Soviet horror.

Normally, a team of two responsible, honorable witnesses is necessary for any decision of a court, but for an *agunah*, a non-Jew or a child or one person who, en passant, offers information about the death of her husband, is considered sufficient for a decision to allow her to remarry. Israel's famous Chief Rabbi, Rabbi Goren, recently settled the case of the Langer family through prolonged, careful, detailed and intimate investigation of the legal facts concerning the mother's marriage.

My own beloved, sainted teacher, the Gaon Rabbi David Hoffman, in the third volume of his Responsa, *Melammed Le'hoil*,[10] solved a most difficult problem of a *Kohen* applying for permission to marry a convert, in an ingenious and compassionate manner.

Dr. Eliezer Berkovits, in his profound book *T'nai Benissuin U'beget*,[11] proposed a way of solving the problem of the *agunah*, which the famous sainted Gaon J. J. Weinberg very warmly recommended.

The latest edition of the *Shulhan Arukh* consists of eight volumes. The new edition, being prepared by the leading scholars of the Holy Land, in cooperation with authoritative sages all over the Jewish world, so far has published fourteen volumes dealing with the first third of the *Even ha-Ezer*, the fourth part of that code.

Problems — of which fifty years ago one did not dream — have aroused the thorough, steadfast interest and study of contemporary authorities: the international dateline and its effect on the Sabbath to its right and left;[11a] artificial change of sex;[11b] Man on the Moon in Halakah;[11c] the dreadful destruction of millions of homes and the disappearance — for years or forever — of husbands, victims of Hitler's and Stalin's bestiality; DNA and its effect on body and mind of human beings; the discovery of the thumbprint to clearly establish a person's identity; new implications of *Dina de Malkhuta Dina* (the obligation to serve the country of one's residence, obey its laws and promote justice and compassion through cooperation in democratic, liberal endeavors).

It is reasonable to assume that the new edition, to be completed by the year 2,000, will have sixty volumes. All through the Rabbinic literature, *Da'at Yahid* (the minority opinion) is quoted so that in doubtful cases, the benefit should be given to the human being, and not to the letter of the law.

In the Supreme Court of America, the original minority opinions of Justices Brandeis and Holmes eventually became the law of the country.

In Israel, the Rabbinic Court, having decided that the husband involved must divorce his wife, upon his refusal to do so, would sentence him to jail or require him to pay a fine large enough to discourage his lack of consideration.

The *Takkanot*[12] (ad hoc regulations) have been part and parcel of our religious literature.

V

What can we do? What is essential for a positive answer to the lib movement? There are three or four items which I recommend to careful consideration of Jewish mothers, teachers, and youth leaders.

When a son is born, the *Brit Milah* is a major event in the family. The daughter's entry into life is mostly ignored, apart from hugs and admiring faces of the relatives. I would suggest some careful consideration of how — within the intimacy of the Jewish home — an arrangement, a ceremony, a kind of gift, could be prepared, about which the growing daughter would later on learn with pride.

At the age of three or four, we give the boy the right to wear tzitzit: "*U'reitam oto u'zekhartem et kol mitzvot haShem* (You shall look upon them, recall all the Lord's commandments and perform your duty)."[13]

The *tzitzit* serve as the boy's perpetual reminder of his Jewish obligations. Nothing like that is being offered to the sweet, young girl. I have discussed matters with a leading person in the Jewish National Fund and asked him to consider the choice of some kind of a necklace, brooch, Menorah, Ten Commandments medallion or pendant, to give the young girl a feeling of belonging, of being appreciated, of having a task and a goal of which the gift is a symbol. He was very enthusiastic and anxious to persuade the Fund's directors to plan the details as soon as possible.[14]

More than three decades ago, I arranged in our Center that every Bar Mitzvah boy be inscribed into the Golden Bar Mitzvah Book of the Jewish National Fund so that the day of his religious maturity ties him with unforgettable ties to the Holy Land. Unfortunately, we have retained almost a monopoly; I am told that very few congregations have followed our example.

27

Of late we have arranged in the dining room of the Center for Bat Mitzvah celebrations, at which time we present the young girl with basic sefarim and with an inscription into the Jewish National Fund Bat Mitzvah Book.

Just as the *tefillin* teach the Jewish boy to think right (*tefillin shel rosh*) as he places them on his head; to wish right (*tefillin shel yad*) as he winds them opposite his heart, and to act right (*tefillin shel yad*) as he places them around his hand, so — in some manner — the wisdom and ingenuity of our women ought to discover a gift that would offer, by implication, by symbol, by encouragement, the same service to the young girl.

All these suggestions are in accord with the *Din Torah* (Jewish Law), its authoritative and ever unfinished code, the *Shulhan Arukh* (The Prepared Table) every new edition of which includes fresh authoritative *takkanot* (regulations, ordinances) and *minhagim* (customs) of our folk throughout the world. The ReMA (Rabbi Moses Isserles, Chief Rabbi of Cracow, rabbinic authority, philosopher and mystic, too) offered his European contribution to the Sephardic *Shulhan Arukh,* and in profound sense of humor, called the new part of the Code, *Mappah* (The Table Cloth).

At the age if 18, *hai* (life) ought to be the watchword symbolized by appropriate ceremony and gift, so that both boy and girl will feel ready, happy and proud to become an important part of the life of the Jewish community.

VI

Throughout the years of parental opportunity, *hinnukh* (Jewish education) must take the form, the spirit and the programme of loving, tender compassion.

Rabbi Akiba's sensitive, inspiring challenge:[15] "If the

husband can find another woman more beautiful than his own wife (that marriage loses its meaning), he should free the latter by divorce." To a normal husband, his wife must remain the most beautiful woman. Only that sainted sage who attributed all his achievement to his beloved mate could have uttered that warning. Almost two millennia later, Robert Ingersoll uttered similar sentiments.

If these matters are given careful consideration, are being translated into abiding, living encouragement, we have reason to believe that the wilderness of a confused, uninformed, unhappy, non-cooperative youth may be conquered for the peace, happiness and happy survival of the Lord's messenger to a peaceless, hungry world.

NOTES

1. Midrash R., Bamidbar II, 2
   Woman (Soncino edition of Jewish Library III)
   Bavli Yebamot 63a, Sanhedrin 49b, Sota 17a, Shabbat 140a
2. Isaiah XXVI, 4
3. Bamidbar II, 2
4. ad locum
5. Bamidbar II, 2
6. So far not identified, but surely based on Bereshith XXXVIII, 3-5, and Ramban's comments.
7. See M. Gaster. *Ketubah*
7a. See my *Rhythm of life*. pp. 131-148, 179-184
8. Mitzvah XIV
9. Yoreh Deah CCXIV, Shibale ha'Leket LXXXI
10. Even Ha'Ezer, VIII
11. Mossad Rav Kook 1967
11a. Noam XIV. M. Kav ha'ta'arikh
11b. Noam XVI. Hithapkut Malakhutit
11c. Ha'adam al Yareah
12. Baba Kama 82a
13. Bamidbar XV, 39
14. Cp., for the total picture, the encyclopedic works edited by Hirsch L. Silverman: "Marital Counselling" and "Marital Therapy" as well as Robert Seidenberg's persuasive "Marriage in Life and Literature,"
      J. D. Epstein "Mitzvot haBayit Judah Licht."
                "Mavo le'Hilkhot Derekh Eretz"
15. B. Gittin 90a

WOMAN'S THREEFOLD ROLE

For a right attitude towards her, there must be a proper appreciation of her function in love, in the home, as educator — three concentric circles.

Love, the most abused and too often least understood of words, has never been more essential than today. Against the deadly menace of maximum destruction by atomic power, there is the maximum source of peace and security which marriage based on love, offers. We all are in need of the warmth, the rousing effect of tender care, the sheer comfort — physical, emotional — flowing from trusted companionship. Nothing can better immunize us against the corroding menace of communal, national, and global conflict (hate-ridden, envy-propelled, despair-sired) as profoundly as a loving wife greeting our homecoming, an understanding husband offering his cheerful comradeship to the mate. The biblical expression "wife of his youth" offers both challenge and counsel. Where there is selfless love, the wife remains throughout marriage the bride, the very sight of whom sets her lover aglow with joy and respect. Woman as lover would, by the grace of her intuition, know her husband's mind and heart, his problems and his harvests. The partners, by their love, would

remain a perpetual source of mutual aid and encouragement. They would achieve a peace and security impervious
to the noise and hazards of the political scene or the market place. Woman has native endowment for love in all its
implications: physical, emotional, mental. She, more than
man, can build married life on what the prophet portrayed
as its four pillars: righteousness, grace, compassion, and
steadfastness (Hosea, 11, 21). Indeed, such love creates a
human summit, it is the fruit of knowing God and loving
Him.

In the gray confusion and ugliness of the super-busy
life, the relentless drive, haste, and friction not only of the
metropolis, but even of smaller cities, American man
needs some vision of harmony, order, relaxing sense of
beauty. The Hebrew *hen* implies all of that (Prov. XXXI,
30). It is a homonym for sympathy, grace, beauty. It requires art, endeavor, patience no less than perception.
Woman's work, but also her wisdom, transforms an
apartment into a home. Woman's unselfish dream goes
beyond period furniture and the latest tricks of T.V. ap-
paratus, into the creation of an atmosphere, the antidote
to the rash, brash, hurried, confused, scene of the street,
into the calming, charming color scheme of her devotion.
Cooking, too, is an accomplishment, with its ingredients of
imagination, attention to detail, appreciative knowledge of
foodstuffs, and consistent application. A good, cheerful
and cheering home is the achievement of woman's devotion and the rock of man's emotional well-being. The husband's success in business or profession may render her
endeavor more pleasant, but the vital, steadfast, step-by-
step progress towards the goal is her own challenge, plan
of work, and eventual triumph.

Love is the basis of wholesome marriage. Grace and the
accomplishment of harmonious home life express the
wife's personality on a level at once practical and romantic.

Both affect the relation between the mates and their heights and depths. Yet, in another sphere, woman's share is utterly more significant — indeed, the decisive element. With noblest effort, the father cannot be a major influence on the emergent character of his children. Because of the incessant demands of his office, study or store, he has neither time, nor mood, neither adequate patience nor sufficient intuition, to be a useful educator. Unless he were to give up his outside work and rely on endowment income, which might free him, releasing energy and granting time, yet not supply him with the wisdom that the loving mother has acquired through pain and understanding, through compassion and dedication. The husband's heart (the book of Proverbs asserts) *trusts* his wife, relies on her to be the potent influence on the children of their love. She teaches them by a hundred details of a kindness and firm righteousness. They see her "stretching out her hand to the poor" (Prov. XXXI, 19) and imbibe at her knee Jewish teaching of social responsibility. The old-fashioned *pushke (charity box)*, into which the old-fashioned mother put her dime before *licht benshen* on Friday night, not only connected the Sabbath feast with mercy, but taught the little ones to include "the poor, the orphan, the widow, the stranger" (Deut. XV, XXIV) in their life's program. The impersonal check mailed at stated intervals to organized charity robs the tender age of the sight, the solid experience of genuine *rahamanut,* and too often the absence of such training results in the ugly type of uncharitable sons of charitable parents: they have no feeling for the underdog and no desire at all to engage in personal effort to help him.

Woman's work is utterly irreplaceable for husband, home, and children. It offers an outlet for all her unspent energies, for her imaginative powers, for her maternal urges. Her esthetic, no less than her ethical urges can find happy fulfillment in her home program. This generation has seen the ebb and tide in the affairs of progressive education. Thirty years ago it was the repressed children of an earlier age who, in heedless reaction, misunderstood its goal to the youngster's self-expression, unrestrained by any earlier value or principle, forgetful of the fact that too often there was no precious self to be expressed. Of late the importance of self-realization has been stressed, and self-discipline as the harvest of wise pedagogy is being universally acclaimed. The home of wise affection — of carefully balanced granting of the child's wishes and equally devoted refusal of unjustified requests — again is the task, the blessing, and the abiding accomplishment of woman's genius.

These are the three roles of woman, trebly precious in our own days, imposing upon her effort, strain, the quality at once of mercy and judgment: She must be the husband's beloved lover, the home's practical, esthetic engineer, the children's living example of goodness, truth, and grace. In the process her *ba'al* (husband) becomes *ishi* (her beloved man), her home a mansion of bliss, her children precious comrades.

KNOWLEDGE AND LOVE IN RABBINIC LORE

Knowledge and love have been from the very inception of Judaism twin goals of individual and collective life. But their foundation throughout has been justice as social morality. *"The righteous man (Tsaddik) is the basis of the world."* The pedagogical device of promised reward and punishment threatened — serving as the means of accustoming men to choose good and shun evil — indicates the universal validity of justice as the vital principle of life, an *"everlasting foundation"* (Prov. X, 25). This is what Moses had taught: *"Judge the people with righteous judgment." "Justice and only justice shalt thou pursue"* (in J. H. Hertz's version) *"that thou mayest live and inherit the land"* (Deb. XVI, 18-20). Judgment, truth, and peace are interdependent: if judgment is executed, truth is vindicated and peace results.

Among the notable encounters with God (*moade Hashem*) reported in the Hebrew Bible are a number of dialogues, from Abraham to Job, each of which deals with one of the aspects of His revelation. The double meaning of Tsedek (both, love and justice, mishpat u-tzedakah) forms the a priori basis for these dialogues. To Abraham, His pioneer ambassador, life without rock-bottom assurance of God's

35

justice, loses all meaning: "*Shall the Judge of all the earth not deal justly?!*" To Moses, our Teacher, only His forgiving mercy will give meaning to his own life: "*Otherwise, blot me, pray, from the book Thou hast written!*" Jonah ben Amittai, the young man on the way to become a prophet, is being shown His all-embracing loving justice and just love: "*And shall I have no pity upon great Niniveh, its myriads of people and its very cattle?*" Despairing Job, unyielding in his plea of innocence and undeserved affliction, learns of His abounding love in the unending panorama of nature, man and beast in His world (XL to XLI).

But it is in the prose paragraphs of Halakhah that the *kaloskagathos* of His fair love shines forth in unique splendor.

Love between husband and wife, to deserve the term kiddushin (sanctity) must partake of both qualities. Occasional overpowering affection is not enough. The Shulhan Arukh insists that there must be not only consent *to* marriage, but, for the dignity of both and the high level of love, there must be consent *in* marriage. In Jewish law the husband's conjugal rights do not include that of approaching his wife without her consent. He must woo her (Eben ha-Ezer XV) throughout the years of married life, only the Am-haaretz (brutal ignoramus) would ever transgress this basic prohibition. The love of fellow man, too, does not envisage a never-never land, a vacation dream of complete abandonment of one's rights and possessions, but fair and loving care. The Hafetz Hayyim, in his "Ahavat Hessed," describes its operation: as the folios of the Talmud and the account books of kehillot, the minutes of congregational or communal meetings (pinkassaot) reveal them. Love of one's fellow men creates such institutions as "Society for Hospitality to Wayfarers," "For Palliative Momentary Help," "Free Loan Society," helping respectable poor over temporary embarrassment, or enabling a craftsman to ob-

36

tain raw materials for the development of his economic security; "Society for the Dowering of Poor Brides," so that they may not grow old with frustration; "The Society for Visiting the Sick," Linat Hatzedek, the society for providing constant vigil at the bedside of persons dangerously ill; The Holy Society for taking care of the dead and providing those who had no relatives or friends with free burial and grave. *Maskil El Dal Society* (literally dealing wisely with the poor) was meant to safeguard the self-respect of the recipient by bestowing its aid in utter secrecy. The Talmud reports about a heedless person offering in public his coin to a needy person. Said the sage who observed it: "You would have performed a greater mitzvah had you not shamed him thus" (Hagigah 10A).

In some communities a beautiful custom served the same purpose. Anyone sitting *shiva* would receive from the office of the local Jewish Welfare Society two boxes, one filled with money, the other empty. The rich would fill the empty one, the poor would empty the full one. The boxes would be sent back to that office, and only the executive official would know what had happened.

Membership in the societies mentioned above was a hallmark of nobility to which every citizen of the Jewish collectivity aspired. Love for the fellowman resulted in market laws and the right of collective bargaining which prevented unfair competition and every form of exploitation, from the Labor Relations Board (*minhag ha-medinah*) already in force in the time of the Mishnah to the ordinances prohibiting the truck system (whose baseness is described in John Steinbeck's "Grapes of Wrath"). Almost two thousand years ago the prohibition of this system and the establishment as recorded by Josephus of the right to a job was an obligation of state and society. In these laws social justice is the matrix and love the creative, crowning element. Rabbinic rules, indeed, present the legal commentary and the concretization of this love-crowned justice and justice-based love.

Gedolah deah shenitnah ben shte otiyot — Great is that knowledge which includes two aspects of God's being: the omniscient power and infinite mercy. Only God has these qualities. *Ke E-l deot Hashem* — God's alone is the power of complete knowledge. Therefore He knows the motivation of actions. As omniscient God, He knows where an act is beneficial without being truly good and when a good act might be stillborn in spite of noble intention. A million dollar building for an orphanage or a hospital may be a beneficial act from the point of view of the many it serves with its skills, its teachers and physicians. But it may not be a good act as far as the giver is concerned, as his motives may have been the expectation of reward, of public approval, or of the acquisition of a good name. God's knowledge composed of both omniscience and mercy will judge the frustrated humanitarian as if he had completed his task. For example, if his plans for similar benefaction miscarried from a sudden change in his financial fortune or from an unwise choice of means, God's merciful knowledge will assess the motivation of the person who does a beneficial act for ulterior motives. By Him attitudes and motivations are valued and accounted.

MAN'S KNOWLEDGE OF GOD

There are three sources within the limits of human capacity of what may be called his knowledge of his Creator. It will be found, however, to embrace His work rather than His essence. Of the latter man knows only that which His revelation has conveyed to him. The cosmos in all its massive beauty, infinite greatness and undeviating conformity to law and order, has given man — both emerging from primitiveness and civilized — a never-failing sense of divine power. The sequence of day and night, winter and summer, sowing and harvesting, as they spell His providence, have widened and deepened the knowledge of His works.

The study of God's mind, where accessible to human questing in progressive intuition as found in the deepest thought of every generation, represents an endeavor to fathom all possible motivations of His law — especially in the *Mitzvot Maassiyot.* Rambam has warned us that our interpretations of the *ta'ame hamitzvot,* encouraging and enlightening as they may appear to us, must never be taken as final or exhaustive of the divine intent. The search in every age opens up new vistas and spurs new endeavor on the road to a wider and deeper understanding. It is the process, no less than the achievement, which is meritorious and promising of ever-greater horizons.

In general, both His Torah, our inferences from the beauty of His world, and the teachings of His prophets and disciples enable us, all distance off the goal notwithstanding, to achieve conviction as to God's moral character, His control of the universe and the purpose of His creation.

Our knowledge of God, however, remains exceedingly insecure wherever individual experience, fate and destiny are concerned. At no given moment can we tell with any degree of certainty the meaning of any particular event in the life of an individual. The finger of God in history will always depend on our reconstructive ingenuity. His very Torah proclaims it: *"And I appeared to Abraham, Isaac and Jacob as God Almighty."* They had seen Him, worshipped Him as the Omnipotent Creator of heaven and earth and human potentialities. *"But in my name as God of history I was not known to them."* It was only generations later that saw the blossoming of His promise, the election of Israel as His ambassador to mankind and the fulfillment of His pledge to bestow the Holy Land upon them. Isaac Arama, in his commentary, thus explains the enigmatic verse, *"Thou shalt see my back, but my face may not be seen"*: Long after figuratively speaking, God has turned His back upon an action or event, man may be able to trace an eventual end result of development, as it were, God's finger in history: the connection between apparently insignificant seed and full harvest. Thus, the dream of Joseph was the first in a chain of divinely planned happenings that brought about exile in Egypt, the revelation of Mt. Sinai, the conquest of Palestine and the vision of the Messianic age.

The Hebrew word for friendship *re-ut* (according to the revelatory verse in the Psalms *Attah yodata shivti vekumi banta be-re-i* literally, *"thou knowest my lying down and my rising up. Thou understandeth my thoughts from afar"*) implies the sharing of ideas and ideals, a type of comradeship in noble causes. But man's love of God can neither be beneficial to Him in the usual sense of the word, nor can we in our terrestrial limitations be said to share anything with Him. It really spells a complete identification with what man considers most important. To illustrate it, I should like to refer to an apparently paradoxical prayer recited by the faithful every morning. It starts thus, *ahavah rabbah ahavtanu. "With great love hast thou loved us. Exceeding mercy hast thou bestowed upon us. Merciful Father, all merciful, have mercy upon us."* After this introduction one would expect something like "Save us from the lion's den. Rescue us from the jaws of death." But what follows sounds anti-climactic: "Have mercy upon us and put it into our hearts to teach, to learn, to observe, to do and to fulfill the mitzvot of your Torah." Why must we implore God's mercy three times for that? The answer lies in the last word of that portion of the prayer — b'ahavah — with love. To learn with love, to teach with love, to fulfill in the love of God, to observe for the love of God. These are rare assets for which we need a special spirit of steadfast dedication. What we really ask for is the divine help to aid us in the quest for complete identification with God's name, in order that whatever we say, do, or fulfill may be a true expression of this utmost devotion. If the supreme form of love is identification with the beloved, so the supreme love of God must be a similar identification. "But God is in heaven and we are on earth and therefore let our words be few." How can we aspire to such identification with Him, no matter how genuine our love is?

To make that point clear we may well use the comment of the Midrash Rabbah on the second verse of the first chapter of the Bible: *veruach E'lohim merahefet al pne*

41

hamayim, which in literal translation means *"The spirit of God hovers over the face of the waters."* Said our sages: *ruho shel Mashiah* literally means, "the spirit of the Messiah." They want to suggest that in the very act of the creation of the world, the Lord had in mind the ultimate achievement, construction, consummation of the world of the Messiah, of a life free from prejudice, envy, hatred and one lived in justice, brotherhood and security. What we are asking in that great prayer is to be given spiritual asset of identification and we also refer to the way it can be achieved: *"enlighten our eyes through Thy Torah— for the love of Thee — an identification with Thy message."* Dabbek libbenu bemitzvotekha, a complete attachment to Thy laws, training us in that identification with the ultimate aim of humanity, the eternal era or realm of righteousness and mercy as the fruit of such consistent effort. *Ve-yahed levavenu* — unite our hearts to love and revere Thy name.

It is the boldest prayer, the most potent quest to our Father in heaven to allow us within the limitation of human nature, that love of complete identification which will spell our own moral fulfillment, happiness, security and achievement of a world which He had planned in the spirit of the Messiah as He created the ineffable boon of light upon cosmos.

There is a basic difference, often ignored, between two states in human relations: falling in love and loving. The first is the result of the sudden impact on one's senses or mind of an enchanting face or figure, of intellectual excellence or, on the lowest level, of material affluence.

To have fallen in love means to have been overcome by that impact to the exclusion, consciously or unconsciously, of every other consideration. How long this state lasts will depend upon the particular personality. It is essentially an ego-oriented condition. Modern Hebrew reveals its essential quality by using the reflexive 'hitahev', normally translated as 'falling in love', but literally meaning 'loving one's self'. The person who has fallen in love has, by ignoring them, abrogated all other facets because he or she expects benefits — physical, spiritual or material, from the person with whom he or she has fallen in love. It is what the Mishna in Abot calls *"Ahavah Teluyah Bedavar"*. The person who has fallen in love may fall out of it when his objective is achieved, may crawl out of it in the progressive stages of disillusionment, may leap out of it by sudden intuition of its worthlessness or as a result of a new powerful stimulus. Falling in love, one may be driven by unbridled desire into excesses of error or extreme. An altogether different state, condition or attitude is that of love. Love implies or pre-supposes a complete evaluation by the lover of the whole personality of the beloved. That sentiment is most likely to be more stable and enduring. It is not due to the upsurge of sudden emotion nor is it overwhelmingly dictated by self-interest. It results in the determination to dedicate one's knowledge, power, and very being to the beloved one. Being in love may be due to either of the two conditions. A superficial man or woman will experience a short period of being in love as he or she recovers from having fallen into it. A deeper one may continue being in love because of genuine dedication to the other person.

The Talmud (Sanhedrin 7a) puts it thus: "When our love was strong we could have slept on the edge of a sword. Now that our love is no more strong, a large abode would not be enough for us."

Love as the expression of identification creates intense loyalty to party, the ideals of which one shares, to the country with whose history and destiny one feels close-ly connected, to universal humanity whose misery (weltschmerz) one is unable to bear, and towards whose peace and happiness one feels impelled to work. The will for unity with all man is the ultimate expression of that identification with the present and the potential high level of peace and happiness of every human being.

God's love of man manifested itself in that He did not present him with a ready-to-use world but with an emergent creation. He bestowed upon him the great blessing and task of being a partner in the work of the beginning. God warned man "to work the earth and to guard it," to use both the raw material He had placed at his disposal and the mind and the skill with which He had endowed him. In the process the world would remove accidental impediments and those due to man's folly or quest for power.

God's love kept the high path toward happiness, security, perfection, before man's mind. The evil consequences which followed upon his abuse of his free will were meant to keep luminous before him the joy and the benefit of following the divine road. Every error of man, every selfish act, every short-sighted plan for self-aggrandizement without care for the improvement of the whole, not only kept man's moral stature down but kept God's world on a lower level.

For man to hear the voice of God and the direction for fulfillment of security and worthwhileness He chose the family of Abraham whose raison d'être should be the proclamation of this right way, who should be a blessing to the world and who should (in Nachmanides' version) graft the ideal upon the physical constitution of mankind. God wanted man to grow with each chapter in the world development. His love gave him a religion not of contentment and relaxation, but of constant challenge. God's love, as it were, was pained by man's zigzag course but though He would let him suffer the consequence of his folly of wickedness, He never allowed the vision of the ultimate to disappear from his view.

When the Chosen People became victims of their human

44

nature and listened to lower schemes of happiness, the Lord sent them His spokesmen (the prophets) whose messages in language both tender and ruthless taught the inevitable consequence of waywardness and the assurance of the eventual end when the earth will be full of the knowledge of God.

The dynamic quality of social imagination is the single hope for the gradual humanization of humanity. The challenge of a peaceful, classless society of brothers and sisters aiding each other out of love and giving each other the benefit of the doubt out of love should be answered through an abiding sense of interdependence bringing about the highest level of human life.

The élite of mankind was ever fired by that imagination and the righteous people among the nations of the world earned divine acceptance by listening to His voice and taking it to heart.

Thus God's love to man extends to all ages through the happy times of contentment as well as the despondency of defeat, never changing its tone, never ceasing its admonition, never diminishing the power of the beauty and sweetness of the ultimate accomplishment of a humane society. To the world of today, God calls to use its ample blessings, its gifts of mind and beauty, its reservoirs of scholars, scientists and research men to bring health and hope to all His children, to raise the submerged two-thirds of mankind to a level where they can fill their vital needs, be assured of their rest, and be happy in the consciousness that back of all the bewildering variety of phenomena is the Rock of Ages, whose voice has sounded from millennia and who will gather His people into His arms of mercy when they are wise and good enough to heed His call, to abolish power dreams, tariffs and immigration quotas to lift the hearts of mankind up to the everlasting hills of God-created, man-earned, man-worked salvation.

God's love for man is permanent, beneficial and ever manifest. Man's love for God is much more difficult of fulfillment. For our normal love takes the form of endearment, tenderness, and of bestowing kindness and benefits. But we cannot bestow any benefit on God. He is above the world of physical things to whom our efforts could bring comfort or aid. Yet in a way He awaits our benefactions. As He created the light of the world, the rabbis said, He had in mind the light of the Messiah. The age of justice, genuine brotherhood, and unlimited love — any move in this direction brings the world of His original vision nearer. There is no noble, gentle, unselfish human attitude lost in His world. Every genuine movement in the direction of His guidance, the Torah, helps to benefit His plan for a happy humanity. No matter how high our scientists will reach in their space flights, they won't be able to practice righteousness or mercy in the inter-stellar space. To love God with all our heart and mind and soul means to be dedicated to the principles and ideals He has given to us in His self-revelation.

His revelation means the uncovering of His character to His children of all ages and climes — the true, the only God as far as human beings can comprehend it. It is manifest in His care and acts of justice and mercy, so that we love God truly by serving justice not for applause or gain or affluence or position, but because they are His qualities.

What we call the ceremonials, what laws and practice serve as symbols, are but a system of training for gradual habituation to righteous and merciful thinking, approaching, and acting.

This love of God binds us to no particular clime, limits us to no particular territory. It raises us above the humdrum meaningless individual world to a level where we act and live in the contemplation of His ultimate goal. As we love His goal, we love Him; as we approach His goal by our consistently selfish effort, we approach Him. As our whole life becomes merged in the chorus of the voices calling for holiness which means reverence, righteousness and mercy, we become merged in the total scheme of things. It is man's tremendous boon to be able to love God and to find his own highest level in the thought and practice thereof.

"The Lord has in this world only the four cubits of Halakhah", that means that God's ideals, His reality become concrete in the life of the individual who serves Him selflessly, nobly, righteously and lovingly.

Righteousness and kindness are mandatory from every human being toward every human being but complete dedication is closest among those held up by the conviction that they are serving together the love of God.

God's love of man expresses itself also in the built-in protection against such accidents as sickness and other mishaps: antibodies, the organic defense against invasion, the immunity against infection such as the medical journals describe in ever-increasing detail. On the principle of *Imitatio Dei,* imitation within the human framework of God's love, we should take care to provide a built-in protection of human happiness, peace and security. It has been, however, our most lamentable failure.

Nearly two-thirds of mankind are still living on a sub-human level. Our capacity for producing food, shelter, education for all human beings is well-nigh unlimited. But our love of man has lagged miserably behind that capacity. Most of the revolutions of bloodshed and hatred of the modern world are due to this stupid selfishness of homo sapiens.

Wherever a catastrophic consequence of indifference to our brother's plight is not properly perceived, impetuous attacks are being made on God's justice "because He allows so much human sorrow." In this connection, an experience of the present writer may not be irrelevant:

A few years ago I had delivered the invocation at an annual meeting of an American medical association. When it was over, a physician, sitting next to me on the dais, said, "Rabbi, this was a beautiful, poetic address, but how can you explain God's love in the light of what we know about the ravages of cancer?" This was my answer: "We are sitting in the financial capital of the richest country in the history of the world. This year's budget for the expenditures of past, and the prevention of future wars, amounted to $47,000,000,000. In the last generation modern research and devotion have succeeded in stamping out most of the deadly diseases that have ravaged mankind. Our annual expenditure for cancer research does not yet amount to $5,000,000. Had we spent one percent of what our budget devotes to war for the establishment and maintenance of institutions for the study of cancer, we might by now, with the help of God and as the harvest of widespread thorough-going effort, have discovered the nature of cancer, its cause and cure. God's love, by endowing us with great mental ability, has provided us with the means of achieving it. We must never permit ourselves to argue against His providence for our failure to live up to His divine command."

"Work this potential Garden of Eden and guard it." For this earth was given to us, not only as a gift but as a task. Today initial plans have been laid for providing future fuel needs by the human race through atomic power. There is as yet another inexhaustible source of energy; that which at present causes the disaster of earthquakes. One of these days human research devoted not to gain alone but to making this world a source of peace and abiding security will learn how to channel the billions of heat energies in the crust of our globe; to provide through them the needs of all God's

48

children who now shiver in cold and suffer the pangs of hunger and are deprived of those vital benefits which the Omniscient, Omnipotent, all loving Father of mankind, has stored in this planet, charging the wisdom, the character and the benevolence of its best minds and hearts to capture, hold and employ for all people.

God's love of man both in its positive and negative aspects still deserves to remain the major concern of mankind.

This love of God for man manifests itself in granting him the capacity for moral judgment. The last chapters of the Book of Job describe His tender care for all life. Undoubtedly, animals have consciousness and awareness, but it is only man that can be aware of harmony, whose artistic sense makes him thrill to a wondrous sunset, achieve profound happiness through Beethoven's symphonies and lose himself in the contemplation of Michaelangelo's Moses.

His imagination describes to him, not only uncharted chapters of his future, but his social awareness creates in him a profound sense of sympathy, empathy and oneness with his fellowman everywhere. His studied judgment creates moral values, truth and beauty from Abraham's blessing for all mankind to the preview of Isaiah's time of the Messiah.

Saadia Gaon eliminated from his Siddur the last lines of the *l'E-l barukh*, the words *or hadash al Tzion ta'ir* (Oh, cause a new light to shine upon Zion), feeling that that prayer was addressed to the Universal Giver of light and should not be narrowed to the light of Zion, no matter how glorious. Saadia was logically right and psychologically wrong, for it has been the genius of our sacred literature to integrate the national with the universal, to find God's love in the beauty — physical or moral — of any human being, in the vision of the ocean of snow-capped peaks on any

49

continent, in the Cedars of Lebanon, in the dew on Mt. Hermon or in the wondrous formation of the mountains near the Dead Sea.

God's love of man manifests itself in his unfolding before us the marvels of His universe, the mathematical perfection of the astral world, the unconquered vista of the Himalayas, the majestic sweep of the Amazon River and the incredible, functional perfection of the human body.

The mystery of pain has evoked deep meditation and has been the subject of many books and pamphlets to justify the ways of God and explain the discipline of sorrow. But the greater mystery is that of utter painlessness. In spite of the elaborate physical and chemical processes involved in food intake, metabolism, digestion and absorption, we suffer neither pain nor discomfort.

God's love of man is especially manifested in the pleasures — physical and emotional — derived from the satisfaction of his biological needs of eating, drinking, sleeping and loving. Childbearing used to be the exception but its pangs promise to be eliminated in the near future by a judicious and skillful use of drugs and program of exercise. (Indeed the original meaning of *be-etzev teldi banim* usually translated as *"in pain shalt thou bring forth children"* in the progressive revelation of the Biblical texts seems due for a new interpretation. The word *etzev* — as seen from a comparison with authentic Arabic philology of the prophetic phrase *habbur atzavim Efrayim* — indicates its root to mean creative, aesthetic work, so that future commentators may translate the verse to read: *"For creative work of fashioning their personalities shalt thou bring forth children."*) But whatever pain parturition has involved in the past was more than compensated for by the ineffable joy the young mother felt as she saw, touched, listened to the sounds of her baby, fruit of her own body that held infinite promise for his future.

God's love of man is shown also in the happiness derived from purposeful work. When Adam was ejected from Paradise, he was profoundly despondent. But, say the rabbis, when he heard the divine order, *"in the sweat of thy brow shalt thou eat thy bread"* his mind became calm and contented. Great is work, says the Talmud, for it honors man as it warms him. From the farmer's deep satisfaction with the harvest of his toil to the scientist's serene contemplation of the stellar world through the instruments he has devised or improved, there is the exquisite happiness of achievement.

For a long time the world view has no more been geocentric. Today we recognize our earth to be only one of the globes, of which there are countless numbers in the intimate galaxies of the world. Man continues to be the center of things. Life is still anthropocentric and will stay so until we are invited to a meeting in outer space of the interstellar academies, including all the imaginable scientists on other planets and stars unless they turn out to be robots equipped with detachable, exchangeable, and illimitable facilities and physical power. We are the heirs and beneficiaries of God's great love which is the source of the ingenuity of human minds and the stirring challenge to the noblest hearts of every age from Moses, Isaiah and Hillel in the Jewish history, to Lincoln, Newton and Gandhi in the larger world.

God's love of man in granting him understanding of spiritual awareness, in keeping him cognizant of classless and warless humanity, inspires him with hope under most adverse circumstances. It helps him to defeat life's shadows by the conviction of an ultimate guiding light.

OF LOVE AND KNOWLEDGE

I

Concerning five kinds of love were the children of Israel commanded in the Holy Torah:

The love of God in Debarim VI, 5

The love of Torah in Jeremiah XVI, 11

The love of the Holy Land in Debarim VIII, 10

The love of the people of Israel in Vayikra XIX, 18

The love of fellow-man in Vayikra XIX, 26.

II

Thou shalt *know* it today and take it to thy heart that the Eternal is The God in the heavens above and on the earth below. There is none else,

The Alenu Prayer of the Siddur.

Thou hast been made to see so that thou mayest *know* that the Eternal is The God, there is none else.

Debarim IV, 35.

53

Thou favorest man with *knowledge* and teachest mortals understanding.

The Amidah of the Siddur

And the earth will be full of the *knowledge* of God even as the waters cover the sea.

Isaiah XI, 9

Immanuel Kant, in his "Theory of Ethics",[1] makes this statement: "Morality is not properly the doctrine how we should make ourselves happy, but how we become worthy of happiness . . . A man is worthy to possess a thing or state when his possession of it is in harmony with the *summum bonum,* (the supreme good). All worthiness depends on moral conduct." "The moral laws lead to religion, i.e., to the recognition of all duties as divine commands." Long before, the first Hebrew, Abraham, had proclaimed justice as the basis of life (*tsaddik yessod olam*), in his bold challenge of his Lord: *"Shall the Judge of all the earth not do justly?"* Without Him, as source and guardian of justice, life has no meaning.[2]

The Kantian over-emphasis on justice implies a denigration of love: "One must live a moral life only out of a sense of duty." In the Torah, justice forms the basic assurance of a minimum to every human being, on which a maximum of *hessed* (kindness) and *rahamim* (unselfish love, literally: mother-love) shall be developed, forming together the synthesis of *Imitatio Dei* (the imitation, within the human frame, of His qualities). The distinction between love not based on justice and the latter as the foundation of the good life is hinted at in Proverbs (XIV, 34): *Justice* (as basis) *uplifts a people, but love of nations* (unsecured as to its objectivity and permanency by justice) *will stay a failure.*

Justice is objective, an all embracing, ever-valid princi-

54

ple, the minimum assurance of fair play and security, the minimum demand for individual worth and collective culture. Justice is not only, as with Thomas B. Macaulay, "far-sighted policy," a type of diplomatic cleverness, statesman-like sound investment or profitable attitude. "Its power is greater and its behest is independent of any one else's reaction." Whether our neighbors repay our own fair treatment of them by righteous dealings with us, or subject us to ruthless power-politics; whether our just behavior elicits similar conduct from fellow humans or not, justice must be pursued at all costs! Even "an eye for an eye"[3] in its original Semitic meaning represents a tremendous advance on the normal heathen reaction which demanded the eyes of all the alien tribe for the loss of one eye sustained by one kinsman. Only *"one tooth for a tooth"* and not the Fascist's "one set of teeth" for one lost by a party member! In Jewish law, however, that ancient phrase *"An eye for an eye"* has a completely different meaning. It stipulates financial compensation for the loss of one eye, for the loss of one tooth. On the basis of justice there must be exact valuation, neither partisan exaggeration of the monetary loss sustained by an insider, nor discriminatory devaluation — of a Negro's, a heathen's, any outsider's damage sustained. The overriding fundamental principle is justice.

On the basis of justice for all, *"the stranger and the home-born, the rich and the poor,"* on the achievement of universal rectitude, one may build up one's personal love, a subjective sentiment. The Torah's timeless teaching: *"ve-ahavta le-reakha" (love thy neighbor)* derives from the constitutional fact *"kamokha"* that *"he is like thee"*, created in the image of God-designed equality, entitled to fundamental, alienable rights and privileges.

"Eye for eye" in Mosaic Law. Further, nothing can illustrate the fundamental difference of the legal systems

55

of these two peoples better than their different application of the law of taliation, or the rule of "measure for measure." The enunciation of the principle of *"life for life, eye for eye, tooth for tooth"*, is today recognized as one of the most far-reaching steps in human progress. It means the substitution of legal punishment, and as far as possible the exact equivalent of the injury, in place of wild revenge. It is the spirit of equity. The Church Father, Augustine, was one of the first to declare that taliation was a law of justice, not of hatred; one eye, not two, for an eye; one tooth, not ten, for a tooth; one life, not a whole family, for a life. The founders of International Law — Hugo Grotius, Jean Bodin, and John Selden — all maintain that the rule "eye for an eye" enjoins, on the one hand, that a fair and equitable relation must exist between the crime and the punishment; and, on the other hand, that all citizens are equal before the law, and that the injuries of *all* be valued according to the same standard. "It is a law appropriate only for free peoples" — said one of the pioneers of modern Bible exegesis, John D. Michaelis — "in which the poorest inhabitant has the same rights as his most aristocratic assailant ... It deems the tooth of the poorest peasant as valuable as that of the nobleman; strangely so, because the peasant must bite crust, while the nobleman eats cake." Of course, in primitive society there was great danger of this principle becoming petrified into a hard and fast rule of terrible cruelty. In the Mosaic Law, however, monetary commutation had already begun. This is seen from the prohibition of accepting money compensation for malicious murder: *"Ye shall take no ransom for the life of a murderer, that is guilty of death"* (Numbers XXXV, 31). The literal application of "eye

56

for eye, tooth for tooth" was excluded in Rabbinic Law; and there is no instance in Jewish history of its literal application ever having been carried out.[4]

Love, as a superstructure on the rock of justice, is capable of tremendous achievement, culminating in self-sacrificing devotion to another human's happiness. Love, as the basis of life, by its very subjectiveness, uncontrolled by the ideal of the summum bonum of righteousness, (the divine principle) would inevitably tend to arbitrariness, according to the taste, viewpoint, prejudices, traumas of the individual, resulting in the Greek scene in Plato's three classes of citizens and in the arbitrary distinctions and discriminations consequent on such classification.

Thoroughly schooled in its disciplines, Jehudah Halevy,[5] in his Kuzari, emphasized the limits of philosophy and castigated the self-satisfaction of his colleagues. The following excerpt from the text of the Kuzari is illustrative:

63. The Rabbi: There is an excuse for the Philosophers. Being Grecians, science and religion did not come to them as inheritances. They belong to the descendants of Japhet, who inhabited the north, whilst that knowledge coming from Adam, and supported by the divine influence, is only to be found among the progeny of Shem, who represented the successors of Noah and constituted, as it were, his (Noah's) essentiality. This knowledge has always been connected with this core, and will always remain so. The Greeks only received it, when they became powerful, from Persia. The Persians had it from the Chaldeans. It was only then that the famous (Greek) Philosophers arose, but as soon as Rome assumed political leadership they produced no philosopher worthy of the name.

64. Al Khazari: Does this mean that Aristotelian philosophy is not deserving of credence?

65. The Rabbi: Certainly. He exerted his mind, because he had no tradition from any reliable source at his disposal. He meditated on the beginning and end of the world, but found as much difficulty in the theory of a beginning as in that of eternity. Finally, these abstract speculations which made for eternity, prevailed, and he found no reason to inquire into the chronology or derivation of those who lived before him. Had he lived among a people with well-authenticated and generally acknowledged traditions, he would have applied his deductions and arguments to establish the theory of creation, however difficult, instead of eternity, which is even much more difficult to accept.

66. Al-Khazari: Now I understand the difference between *E-lohim and Adonai*, and I see how far the God of Abraham is different from that of Aristotle. Man yearns for Adonai as a matter of love, taste, and conviction; whilst attachment to E-lohim is the result of speculation. A feeling of the former kind invites its votaries to give their life for His sake, and to prefer death to His absence. Speculation, however, makes veneration only a necessity as long as it entails no harm, but bears no pain for its sake. I would therefore, excuse Aristotle for thinking lightly about the observation of the law, since he doubts whether God has any cognizance of it.

III

Hasdai Crescas,[6] connoisseur of both Aristotle and his disciple Maimonides, offered trenchant criticism of the former and affectionate disagreement with the latter.

58

"Many of our people have presumed a vision in dreams and foreign vanities. Even the great ones among our sages have been attracted to their (the philosophers') words and have adorned themselves with their arguments and proofs. Among them the sublime master, our Teacher, Rabbi Moses ben Maimon, who, notwithstanding the greatness of his mind and his all-embracing knowledge of the Talmud, found good reasoning in the works of the philosophers and their statements. Indeed, they enticed him, so that he made of their weak premises veritable pillars and fundamentals of the Torah.

I should like to make clear however that the Master does by no means oppose the bases of the faith. But whilst we love his words and even his causeries, we love truth more!" (From the introduction to his magnum opus.)

In Halevy's animadversions, as in Crescas' respectful strictures, the basic point of discussion was the relation between knowledge and love in man's association with his fellow man, as well as in man's connection with his Creator.

To the categories of *Shilton Ha-Sekhel* (the rule or primacy of the intellect) and *Shilton ha-Yosher* (the rule or primacy of righteousness), one might fitly add *Shilton ha-Ahavah* (the rule or primacy of love) as they appear in that perennial debate.

In the sacred literature of our people, prophecy complemented the work of the intellect. Intellect alone would never have penetrated even the periphery of the mystery of God. Only through the sources of divine love was the prophet able to gain an understanding of ultimate verities and ethico-spiritual values. Crescas' *"Or Adonai"* complements Rambam's *"Moreh"* and *"Deot"* alike. In the dramatic midrashic elaboration of the verse in Mishle (Proverbs),[7] God consults the Torah before the creation of the world (potentially the fulfillment of His plan for the humanization of humanity). Was it an academic consultation on the divine level? Or was it divine social engineering? Or, was there the pre-vision of *Hashgahah peratit* (Providence), guiding man, without forcing him, in the direction of ultimate messianic harmony?

The intellectualist Rambam did not envision the problem as Crescas embraced it: "To the omniscience of the perfect God, no particular 'purpose or project' could have arisen at any particular time." In the Maimonidian coinage, such a positive attribute of God would have been implied in our attempt to comprehend His 'project' and would therefore ascribe anthropomorphic qualities to Him.[8]

Crescas sees creation as an endless process and infinite harvest of His love. Indeed, the *"Imitatio Dei"*, (The Imitation of God) which the Torah demands, described only the attitude of such creative love towards every one of His children. Such creative love, an emanation of God-like power, of the God-like property of every soul, knows no limitation, geographical, racial, or social.

Rav Ashi had that in mind, when, in reaction to R. Hamnuna's anger against Babylonian oppressors of his people, he confessed: "I do not understand my colleague's sentiment; I bless them all, Jews and non-Jews, even the cruel heathen."[9]

Crescas quoted both commandments: *"Thou shalt love the Lord thy God"*[10] and *"Thou shalt know Him"*[11] and did not hesitate to ascribe primacy to the first, even as Rambam did not hesitate to define it in intellectual terms, called much later the "intellectual love of God."

Thomas Aquinas, who, through his teacher, Albertus Magnus, owed much to Rambam,[12] nonetheless followed Crescas in his declaration that to love God is better than to know Him. When Diotima[13] told Socrates that love is a philosopher, she may have essayed a compromise. Plato's "symposium" stressed with precious clarity that just as the lover craves harmonious union with the one he loves, so does the "knower" seek intellectual union with the subject of his knowledge.

The Hebrew language, through encouragement of the full apprehension of *one* word, suggests the depth of the problem. *"Heahez"* means to "possess something" and to "be possessed" by it: as one reaches mastery of affection or apprehension, one is mastered by the object involved. How poor, in comparison, sounds Aristipp's boast about the woman of his love: *"Echo ouk echomai* — I have but I am not had."[14]

The rabbis, from the time of the Mishnah to the author of *"Hafetz Hayyim"* of our century, have striven to achieve knowledge as love of God, even as they have endeavored, in their personal lives and letters, to know their fellow-men and to love them.

The relation between these two, love and knowledge, is the subject of the present study and may, perchance, serve as an epilogue to "Men of the Spirit," the last of the three biographical volumes of "The Jewish Library."

The knowledge of God may come as the result of contemplation, prolonged and concentrated; as an appreciation of His infinite wisdom, derived from the phenomena and processes of His infinite world; as an intuitive revelation, vouchsafed in moments of ecstasy; as the harvest of devout immersion in the timeless texts of our sacred literature. King David found such knowledge in the marvelous order of the astral world (*"When I behold thy heavens, the work of thy hands . . ."*).[15] Rabbi Israel Meir ha-Cohen of Radin (the saint and sage, venerated as the author of *"Hafetz Hayyim"*, one of the noblest works of rabbinic literature) cherished it as the spirit of the Lord, revealed in the sublime level of Jewish social ethics.[16]

61

Neither mind nor heart, unaided, could offer enough light in the quest for such knowledge. Only the combination of intellectual and emotional approaches, within their limitations, could lead to some rewarding goal in the progress towards *Da'at Elokim* (the knowledge of God). The mind would search for every avenue that may widen or deepen the horizon for an ultimate comprehension of the glory of God, while the heart would crave a vision of His justice, mercy, and creative love to bless its hopes, stir its resolves, and spur its ceaseless longing for an embracement of His spirit.

One may, by painstaking study of the character and personality of another, reach such total appreciation of the object of his thought, that the ensuing predictability of his conduct, crowning the original appreciation, leads to a relationship that may be termed "love." Thus the sentiment of love may be derived from a profound and steady awareness of a strong, noble character. Frequently, love springs from the synthesis of intellectual admiration and emotional acceptance. Abstractly, one person may love humanity; concretely, one individual may love another. Abstract emotion is found in the happy affection an adult feels for childhood, since this represents in charming form a universal group experience during which there is a feeling of man's infinite potentiality. The optimistic prediction would emphasize the hope that under normal circumstances the children will become adults possessed with ultimate moral and spiritual decencies. Moreover, the love of children generically or the love bestowed upon an individual youngster, frequently presents a compensatory expectation of personality fulfillment, most salubrious to the sorrow of one's private or public frustrations.

Normal love between men and women has intellectual or emotional roots and represents personality appreciation.

The question of primacy is not vital, because a simultaneous inner movement towards total affection, in which both share, is quite within the range of possibility. The highest form of love between members of different sexes has both elements that are bridged by the unity of ethical or spiritual values. This unfailingly results in a camaraderie, engendered by the endeavor to achieve these values, whether they be academic, social, patriotic, or artistic. The unavoidable resignation of mature persons may often be due to deep awareness of the discrepancy between their actual position and the goal towards which they are striving. However, as they work together toward that distant goal, their attachment for each other is deepened. Potent intellectual or emotional elements may manifest themselves as the man and the woman become immersed in their reverence for the cosmos, the shared Socratic *daimonion,* or the revelation of the interdependence of human happiness, justice and eternal peace. Intuitive awareness of the uncharted regions of a man's or woman's personality may open up a vista, a total or vital comprehension which would be denied to any piece-meal search of a probing mind. The Greek *"prosopon"*[17] presumes a universal human type, whose naturalized form, the Jewish *"partzuf"*,[18] in the rabbinic adage, insists on the utter uniqueness of every child of God. Therefore, before one can accept or reject a fellow human being, he must have an understanding of him. So that, knowledge and love would appear postulated as partners.

Love may move from the level of sex attraction to the selfless devotion of *"rahamanut"* or "motherliness," which seeks to spend its powers, understanding, and knowledge for the benefit of the helpless infant; it may grow from passionate desire to passionate self-sacrifice. As *Imitatio Dei,* such *rahamanut* is accorded the supreme quality of

Kedushah or holiness, whose ingredients are reverence for personality, righteousness of act and attitude, and the crowning glory of mother-love.

What Seneca had proclaimed about knowledge: "Were wisdom granted to me on condition that I keep it to myself, I would refuse it!", applies doubly to the quality of love. Baco of Verulam's *"Tantum enim possumus quantum scimus"* (our potency is limited to our knowledge), could fitly be applied to love: only insofar as we love, do we understand God or man or even animals. For *rahamanut* (unselfish motherly love) extends to all life. Knowledge may be the result of search propelled by love and the Talmud emphasizes[19] the consequence: the prohibition, on biblical authority, of any unnecessary infliction of pain on the animal, for *"His mercies are over all His creatures,"*[20] the decisive word *"rahamav"* emphasizing the devoted care that would prevent cruelty to any living thing.

IV

The knowledge of God has been the perennial subject of philosophical and theological interest.[21] Its relation to the love of Him has challenged and enchanted commentators on Holy Writ, students of the Talmud of all ages and, in particular, the masters of medieval Jewish thought, as well as scholars of the last few centuries. The "marvel of self-love" has been investigated also by the great teachers of Hassidism, with *Israel Ba'al Shem Tov* at their head. How remarkable is the devotion, the indefatigable sustained effort of an individual for what he considers his welfare! Yet he is not unaware of his shortcomings, of the trickery he employs in the advance of his aims, of the uncontrolled temper he displays when he even only suspects an assault on his possessions or his dignity or his comfort. "This is the meaning of the radical law, *'Love thy neighbor as thyself'*,"[22] said Rabbi Israel. "Ignore his shortcomings as you ignore your own! Go to all lengths to excuse, or explain, or account for, his action or attitude which at first displease you, even as you find reasons, excuses, justifications for your own acts or attitudes which obviously are far from right! Try to know him in his frailty as you know yourself, and thus extend love to him!"

The love of man for woman is referred to in the fourth chapter of Bereshith in these words: *"And Adam knew his wife Eve and she became a mother and bore a son."*[23] They have ever been animadverted on, illustrated and compared with biblical texts on this subject. The mystic adumbrations of Torah and prophet, the symbolical interpretations of the "Song of Songs", the sage and reverent observations of the rabbis in Talmud and Midrash, have all deepened and broadened the understanding of love. But, above all, it has been the relation of man's love for woman and his understanding of her, in their interpenetration, that have challenged and enriched the searcher and have been of enduring influence upon thoughtful lovers and students of love in all ages.

In the fabric of the patterns of religious life, there has been an unchanging analogy: love of man, knowledge of fellow man, of man for woman and woman for man on one level, and love of God, knowledge of God, understanding of His way with man, on the higher one.

Righteousness as the law of life (in all nuances: from conformity to moral law to a steady endeavor to bridge the gap between the legal paragraph and the postulates of equity) depends on some basic knowledge of both matter and manner, some fundamental understanding, even in every business enterprise. The technical term again is *da'at*, meaning, literally, "knowledge" and spelling here "agreement as to fundamentals," a meeting by the minds of purchaser as well as buyer as to their intention and mutual desire to consummate the deal on the basis of shared knowledge and understanding as to what, when, and how, is to be sold.[24] Such *da'at* is essential also for the validity of labor-contracts, as of communal, national or international negotiation.[25] The very term *"re'a"* (fellowman), one of the major contributions of our sacred heritage to the common treasury of man and at the very base of the Torah's social ethics, etymologically implies community of thought, *da'at*.[26] The knowledge of the human situation, conveying sympathy through empathy, is meant to lead to concrete measures, in law and social custom, for the correction of communal abuses and the promotion of communal harmony. The obligation to remain conscious of this goal as well as of the well-nigh impassable distance of its achievement, is meant to offer challenge and promise to those of His children as love the Lord of the universe and seek to know the Father of every human being.

V

To seek to know the mind of God, asserts Saadya[27] amounts to no less than to seek to be God. For His mind and His knowledge are not only quantitatively but especially qualitatively different from, and unreachable by, human beings. The emphasis on His moral qualities, as revealed in the Theophanies which Moses, Isaiah, David, and Job, were granted, prepares for the interrelation, if not interdependence, of knowledge and love.

Which is primary? In the deepest sense, one ensues from, encourages the other. Love serves as a fountain of intuition, cognition, growing awareness, occasional ecstatic vision.[28] Knowledge seeks the nearness, penetrates the approach, yearns for concrete embracement, of His mind, His infinite goodness, His pervading and elusive Essence. For the interhuman situation, there is a fascinating analogy, in man-woman seeking, knowing, loving. In the light of that analogy, the timeless interpretation of the "Song of Songs" as a dialogue between the loving, searching bride, the chosen people, and the loving God as Israel's Friend and Guide, as Creator of their philosophy of life, seems less abstruse and evidences a deeper comprehension of that identification than millennial epistemological adventures have ever achieved.

All the mystery of the human personality notwithstanding, an ultimate understanding between loving husband and wife is well within the realms of probability.

Here love and knowledge result in an interpenetration of emotional and intellectual fulfillment. But in the other realm, that of God-seeking, God-loving, God-knowing, there remains an unbridgeable gap because of which full achievement stays beyond the levels, no matter how high, of the human mind. The *Imitatio Dei* even in the moral and spiritual sphere, is the supreme goal that can but summon His children, which they, indeed, feel bound to reach for, but the complete attainment of which, by even their noblest, wisest, deepest personalities, stays impossible. However, it is never a hopeless enterprise, for the very process of that quest exerts profound influence on the devout climbers towards the peak of that "mountain of the Lord." There remains a solid good: whilst a perfect human personality has not as yet appeared, the search for God, on the wings of love for Him, may extend and deepen, far beyond present levels, a vision or even a calm perception of the absolute, perfect, timeless Being.

Man will be forced to resign himself to the great gap between him and the knowledge of God, His nature or His essence.

VI

Genuine love implies self-identification with the beloved.[29] It is empathy in its deepest form. Total response to another releases intuitive energies, opens up new horizons, and leads to a fuller knowledge of an essence than otherwise possible. The intimate relation between the object seen, the act of seeing, and the personality of the observer,[30] may serve as illustration, however imperfect. In the confluence of intellectual and emotional love, through the interaction and interdependence of the persons, or person and object, involved, the frontiers of love and knowledge coalesce.[31] On that level, the love of God and the love of one's fellow human, including the love between members of the two sexes, invite analogy, if not identification. Both the mystery and the rational approach are found in Ibn Ezra's interpretations of the Song of Songs, a non-theological, but philosophical and philological reading of that *megillah*.[32]

The love of the adult for an infant derives not only from the wonder of its body, its incipient movements, its efforts to penetrate with tiny fingers into reality, but from conscious, half-conscious, or unconscious identification, to some degree, with the infinite potentialities of every baby; partly as compensation for one's frustration,[33] as inchoate hope for the solution of the problems perceived in maturity, but more so out of realization of the need to resign oneself to a distance off one's own goals and to attach oneself to as yet unspelled-out expectation that the chances for self-fulfillment or self-realization will increase for the personality unfolding with the infant's every hour. The contemplative awareness of this untapped energy, not-yet-arrived opportunity, of his emergent intellectual and emotional riches, becomes a subterranean source of the emotional energies which feed the love of general and individual infancy and childhood. Here again, the line between intuition and rational enterprise is thin, indeed, and they promote each other.

Mature love between the sexes, too, is the fruit of knowledge: first a kind of revelation of personality, conveyed through eyes, ears and the thinking processes which eventually integrate sensation into judgement. Just as vision, appreciation and depth-knowledge of character call forth love, so is the search for knowledge that is comprehensive and penetrative the fruit of love.

The passionate and persistent seeking of a deeper apprehension of God's attributes as accessible to human search and yearning, has its human counterpart in the zealous exploration of every facet of the beloved person, so that love may end and reach fulfillment in the full knowledge of, dedication and surrender of one's self to, the beloved. For the interpretation of this total search, the languages and the images of philosophy, poetry, mystic vision and rational definition, are complementary. Only the sum of all the ways of love and knowledge in search and aid of each other, will represent the whole beauty and power of the polar tendencies meeting in the mystery.

The normal assumption that knowledge leads to love has its variations from Plotinus's ecstatic vision to Bergson's intellectual sympathy.[34] The awareness that love leads to knowledge has its mystic approach as well as its erotic assertion. The Biblical *"And Adam knew his wife Eve and she bore a child"* has evoked the latter interpretation. The translation of Socrates' Ethos into Plato's *logos*[35] stimulated similar consideration. The vision of transcendent beauty is as much the fruit of the former as of the latter. In the myths of the latter's dialogues and epistles, the two realms are at least adumbrated, at best portrayed with rare insight and brilliance.[36] It is knowledge which opposes sophistry through the love it begets. It is love which encourages the search for the *summum bonum,* the vision of which has rendered it more dynamic.[37] The pursuit of both is an ongoing process, a *birkhat gomlim,*[38] *hashpa'at gomlim,* impervious, on its proper level, to both the cynic's sport and the boor's clumsiness. The good and the beautiful may be reached by parallel ways meeting in the infinity of the *kalos-kagathos.* The platonic opposition to dualism and to a superficial monism seems to stress the essential need of this checks-and-balances program on the way towards knowledge leading to love and based on knowledge.

Max Scheler[39] quotes Goethe's dictum: "One does not acquire knowledge except of that which one loves, and the deeper and fuller the knowledge is to become, the stronger, more powerful and more vivid, must the love thereof, yea, the passion thereof be," and Leonardo da Vinci stated that love is the daughter of a great perception (intuition or knowledge). The primacy varies from the former to the latter. Pascal[40] on grounds as emotional as philosophical, identifies love with reason. Judgments as to ethical primacy, too, will affect the cause and effect suggestion in the achievement. (Scheler's brief but profound essay on the subject should offer fresh light, although his interpretation has some neophyte tendencies in need of correction.)

The Hebrew *"heahez"*[41] as indicated above, suggests that we possess what we love and are possessed thereby, a pregnant interpretation of the mutuality of the love-knowledge relation.

Erotic love, a source of perpetuation, may promote the chances of perfect knowledge through the observation of the child's movement towards refinement, the increasing perception thereof strengthening the lover's awareness, assets, and position. The "collective unconscious" of Carl G. Jung,[42] the Hindu idea of love as the intellectual recog-

70

nition of the unity of being,[43] the trend towards each other of the lovers' originally unseparated entities, all represent nuances in the search for expression of the primeval relation. One may perchance find anticipation of this idea in the Midrashic concept of the original andro-gynic man.[44]

VII

Man in his love of God seeks to complement his own happiness by more knowledge through love, more love through increasing knowledge. But God's love of man, as recorded to Moses, as emphasized by the prophets and by their disciples, the Sages of the Agadah, has only one purpose: the promotion — without determinative affecting of his freedom of will — of man's happiness through increasing perfection of character and personality. The divine element in man is to lead not only the individual Jewish soul towards ever higher levels, but to aid every fellowman in such an upward climb. The supreme human vision of God will hence be achieved not by intellectual effort, but through identification with, dedication to, and consistent striving after, God's aim for the happiness and moral self-realization of man. That principle has been the essence of Jeremiah's radical assertion: all search for the essence of God must remain ever unsuccessful, both, because of the limitations of the human mind and the utter inaccessibility, to time-and-space-bound endeavor, of the Creator. No world-escaping hermit is granted a deeper vision, no philosopher worshipping the Absolute, can penetrate the mystery of His being. The knowledge of God, within the frame of human potentiality, is achievable only through the imitation of His ethical qualities conveyed through His revelation, even Justice and Compassion. The word "Tzedek" is a homonym, including both. Both are manifested by the assumption and discharge of social responsibility, by dynamic, wise love of one's fellow-man, by loving identification with his problems and by empathy with his fallible weakness. Righteousness governs not only one's actions as to personal honest, normal juridical relations, it also stirs up and sustains profound indignation, protesting and battling every manifestation of *"hamass"* (violence or oppression in any form). Compassion again creates and sustains attitude and conduct on the levels of *"Lifnim mishurat ha-Din* (generous equity)," *"Kiddush hashem"* (morally sublime action inspired by the purpose of sanctifying His Name — a unique and supreme Jewish virtue), *"ahavat hinnam"* (general love of humans without specific cause, gratuitous love), because of one or all of which a person would forego his or her legal or technical advantage for the love of God and man, the fruit at once of pure altruism and pure worship of God.

One will never know God through either mere intellectual endeavor, or through mere emotional identification with His spirit. It is only by passionate love of and work for the widow and the orphan, the alien and every one else who is underprivileged that one's knowledge of Him may reach the human peak. There were the twelve precious jewels attached to the four rows of the breast plate of the High Priest. The Four Turim (rows or volumes) comprising the totality of Jewish law find their crowning complementation in The Hoshen Mishpat, "The Breastplate of Justice," the last part of the authoritative but ever unfinished "Prepared Table" (Shulhan Arukh), Rabbi Joseph Karo's Code.

Righteousness alone, all its assets notwithstanding, will not bring about, nor express, full knowledge or love of Him. Just as epistemology, with all its keen and wholesome insights, as its ultimate harvest, offers essentially but a sense of our mental limitations, so mere righteousness does not encompass the full program of the Holy Torah. Optimistic views as to cause and effect in political affairs may endorse the merit, essential and timeless, of right conduct. It is true that to the student of the Torah justice is much more, indeed, the basic principle of religion of the good life it enjoins and inspires. Nor is it necessary to emphasize again that without justice neither religion nor human existence are left with any meaning. But justice is only a basis and its very flowering depends upon the steady functioning, in thought, sentiment and practical conduct, of other ethical potencies.

VIII

It is the expected mutuality of justice which we have recognized as at once its major asset and its major liability. For teaching "*Tzaddik yessod olam* (the righteous is the foundation of the world)" in all its interpretations abounding in rabbinic literature emphasizes that even if no mutuality were expectable, even when the just person would meet with dismaying ingratitude or unrighteous response to his righteous action, for him the principle must retain all its pristine cogency and power and his actions must remain righteous and compassionate. On the common level, as a mere wise policy, we have seen it as essentially selfish because reward-promising. Since Bahya ibn Pakudah we have accepted his position, i.e. that for the development and achievement of an ethical personality one must recognize rewards and punishments, with all their solid attractiveness and deterrent effect respectively, as but a device of an educational method for the morally as yet immature, most intelligible and appreciated in the light of the Aristotelian principle of the process of habituation, but both non-vital consequences of conduct and both of negative effect on the fruition of moral ideals.

The just person who is aware and hopeful of proper reaction to, or reward for his equitable and/or charitable deeds, does not possess a knowledge of God's character, sufficiently dynamic to achieve the requisite quality and measure of *Imitatio Dei*. For God's mercy is self-propelled, an expression of His moral Being, absolute, because above any expectancy of reward or possibility of benefit or improvement through such recompense for His goodness and justice. The prophet Isaiah proclaimed it in one verse (50a): *"Ha-e-l ha-kaddosh nikdash bitzedakah"* — The Holy God is sanctified by His righteousness.

It is only through dedicated attention to the helpless, the sick, the forlorn, that fuller awareness of His goodness is evidenced. It is only when the human act or attitude is "absolute," which, in this context, above all means "independent of, above and untouched by," any positive or negative reaction that man reaches out towards His revealed quality.

Finally, this knowledge of God is the only true chance for self-knowledge. As striving and triumphant, or defeated and frustrated, angry or satisfied humans, we know only part of our own potentiality. A mother, genuinely *rehamanah,* discovers bottomless qualities in herself. Serenity is the fruit of the pleasure of a good deed. The patient attitude and consistent loyalty in performing a good deed opens up new horizons of one's personality, and reveals new depths of understanding. Intellectual achievement, too, gives one pleasure. Emotional excitement has its own satisfactions, but the consciousness of having succeeded in solving the problems of one's fellow man by our unselfish endeavor, of having corrected his errors with a minimum of embarrassment and a maximum of encouragement for him, widens and deepens one's sense of human interdependence and quickens one's *joie de vivre.*

It is the creative quality of mercy that crowns justice and through the buoyant effect on fellow-man, reveals his, as it does one's own, fuller stature.

There seems to be a congenital inconsistency in many thinkers. Speaking in rabbinic terms: they will reject on principle as *pshat*[51] (*simple* meaning of the text), what they will admit as *derash* (homiletical or ad hoc interpretation). In the effort to establish the simple text meaning, for the definition of principle, they will often be harsh and uncompromising philologists, only to employ the emotional, homiletical, metaphysical interpretation in another connection. Elsewhere[52] I have shown in connection with R. Simeon bar Yohai's interpretation of Genesis VI, 4. One may find it in R. Jacob Emden's apparently ambivalent attitude to the book of Zohar.[53] I should like to point out a not too dissimilar phenomenon in the fifth book of Spinoza's Ethics as compared to his strictly mathematical method in the rest of his book. An interesting instance may be found as one compares Rambam's Moreh, III, 51 with the note at the end of chapter 54.[54] As against the emphasis on the intellectual love of God in the former, the last part of the classic work stresses the knowledge of God through the contemplation and imitation of His ethical qualities.

This is how the text reads in Friedlander's accurate translation:[55]

> "We are thus told in this passage (Ex. XXXVIII) that the Divine acts which ought to be known, and ought to serve as a guide for our actions, are *"hesed* (loving-kindness)," *"mishpat,* (judgment)" and *"tzedakah* (righteousness)". The object of the passage is to declare that the perfection in which a man can truly glory is attained by him when he has acquired — as far as this is possible for man — the knowledge and

love of God. Having acquired this knowledge, he will then be determined always to seek loving-kindness, judgment, and righteousness and thus imitate the ways of God."

In his *"Iggeret ha-Kodesh,"*[56] Rabbi Shneur Zalman of Liady states that *Tzedakah* in its other meaning: charity is the greatest of all the mitzvot and that[57] Israel will be redeemed only through (the practice or merit of) Tzedakah; that the love of God flows from the very depth of the heart and is superior to knowledge (of Him).

IX

Rambam's emphasis on the knowledge of God as the primary duty of the faithful[58] and Shneur Zalman's stressing of Tzedakah as the noblest *mitzvah,* (commandment, good deed), represent two apparently, though not necessarily, contradictory views.[59]

The prophet, as God's spokesman, makes timeless pronouncements. The faith in, as the mystery of, their origin will remain an ever-dynamic source of metaphysical discussion. But their message has been found applicable in all lands, with all configurations, social, religious, local or universal.[60]

The philosopher — for enlightenment or criticism — sums up the meaning of events or systems of thought and endeavors to include all nuances and facets for a complete statement.

The pietist probes to the very depth of human potentiality. He is profoundly aware and humbly conscious of Divine power, and of the benign wisdom and abiding unity in the changeless source behind the various aspects of the universe. The philosopher's definitions as well as the pietist's intuitive reactions to the validity of these definitions have often been foreshadowed by the prophetic message.

What the philosopher achieves as the fruit of prolonged meditation or fast bold abstraction, what the pietist finds in his self-abandonment to the One, the Eternal, the source at once of meaning, hope and challenge, the prophet, in cases without number, has long ago summed up in his "*Thus said the Lord*" revelations.

Maimonides, in the first and second chapter of *Hilkhot Yessode ha-Torah* (The laws concerning the basic Principles of the Torah) makes the following statement:

"The fundamental of all the basic principles, the pillar of all sciences, is to know that there is a First Being who brought all existing things — celestial, terrestrial and intermediate — into being, and that all of which exist only because of His own real existence. One will be led to love and reverence of Him through the contemplation of His great and wondrous works and creatures, which affords one a glimpse of His incomparable, limitless wisdom. The Torah expresses this thought in its text: '*There is none besides Him*,'[61] i.e. no being truly like Him. Did not David say: '*When I behold thy heavens, the work of thy fingers — what is man that thou art mindful of him and the son of man that thou thinkest of him?*' In accord with these words, I shall explain the works of the Sovereign of the Universe that they may serve the man of discernment as a door to the love of God. For, this God, honored and awesome, it is our duty to love and revere."

To seek to know God, in the view of Maimonides, is the supreme, the first and foremost mitzvah (command or good deed). There are two ways for fulfilling it. One is the study of nature. The Talmud[62] puts it thus: "One who knows the science of cycles and planets (astronomy) and does not follow it, concerning him Scripture says: '*But they regard not the work of the Lord, neither have they considered the operation of His hands.*'"[63] The other pathway is the study of His revelation, the *Torah* (or guidance) to goodness, worthwhileness, happiness and peace. In particular is it the process of the study of *Taame ha-Mitzvot* (the possible motivation of His commandments) that may grant one a glimpse of the divine mind. Hence Rambam's pre-occupation, especially in the third book of his *Moreh Nebukhim* (Guide of the Perplexed), with the search for the motivation of every Mitzvah, in which a human being may seem to catch a reflection of His set of values and ideas. Such discovered "cause" however, no matter how fascinating to the particular searcher, is but the fruit of his individual investigation and must not be assumed to be the ultimate or full divine motive. Nor may conformity to His mitzvot ever be made dependent on the discovery of some personally satisfactory reason. Therefore the search for an ever fuller, deeper apprehension of His unfathomable mind remains the supreme Mitzvah and the resulting *Shilton ha-Sekhel* (no matter how far from the ultimate goal) one of the greatest consummations achievable by His loyal ambassador to the rest of mankind: the studious, steadfast students of the Torah among all the children of Israel. The accent throughout is on intellectual endeavor, although its rigid insistence is relaxed in the last chapter of the Moreh.[64]

"The prophet does not content himself with explaining that the knowledge of God is the highest kind of perfection; for if this only had been his intention, he would have said, "*But in this let him who glorifieth himself, find glory, that he understandeth and knoweth Me,*" and would have stopped there, or he would have said, "*that he understandeth and knoweth Me and knoweth Me that I am One,*" or, "*that I have not any likeness,*" or, "*that there is none like Me,*" or a similar phrase. He says,

78

however, that man can only glory in the knowledge of God and in the knowledge of His ways and attributes, which are His actions, as we have shown (Part I. liv.) in expounding the passage, "*Show me Thy ways*" (Exod. XXXVIII. 13). We are thus told in this passage that the Divine acts which ought to be known, and ought to serve as a guide for our actions, are, "*hessed,* (loving-kindness)," "*mishpat,* (judgment)," and "*tzedakah,* (righteousness)." Another very important lesson is taught by the additional phrase, "*in the earth.*" It implies a fundamental principle of the Law; it rejects the theory of those who boldly assert that God's providence does not extend below the sphere of the moon, and that the earth with its contents is abandoned, that "*the Lord hath forsaken the earth*" (Exod. VIII. 12). It teaches, as has been taught by the greatest of all wise men in the words, "*The earth is the Lord's*" (Exod. IX. 29), that His providence extends to the earth in accordance with its nature, in the same manner as it controls the heavens in accordance with their nature. This is expressed in the words, "*That I am the Lord which exercise loving-kindness, judgment and righteousness in the earth.*" In a similar manner we have shown (Part I. liv.) that the object of the enumeration of God's thirteen attributes is the lesson that we should acquire similar attributes and act accordingly. The object of the above passage is therefore to declare, that the perfection, in which man can truly glory, is attained by him when he has acquired — as far as this is possible for man — the knowledge of God, the knowledge of His creatures in their production and continued existence. Having acquired this knowledge he will then be determined always to seek loving-kindness, judgment, and righteousness, and thus to imitate the ways of God."

An apparently contradictory emphasis is found in the writing of Lubavitch, Rabbi Shneur Zalman of Liady. He does stress the love of God as a primary commandment, and following earlier thinkers, bases it on a sense of gratitude for His endless bounty, but his major praise is unconnected with the processes of an inquiring mind or the results of such uninterrupted quest. He quotes the sages of the Talmud[65] who insisted: We must be more careful about the mitzvah of Tzedakah (charity) than about any other positive commandment, for it is of importance equal to all the Mitzvot of the Torah,[66] and brings redemption nearer.[67] Not a cloistered hermit, but a dynamic shepherd of his people, Rabbi Shneur Zalman had learned about the pangs of poverty so that the potent expression in the Talmud about the merit of relieving it had his comprehensive understanding. He found fault with earlier and contemporary teachers whose praise of the silent, solitary life, dedicated to worship of God, to the contemplation in utter loneliness of His greatness and mystery, had dimmed their sense of the glory of Tzedakah, quick, delicate, warm aid to the suffering. They knew too little about the misery of the masses who lived shut out from comfort, and unable to supply their primitive needs. More than once did Shneur Zalman forsake his court for lengthy visits to the drab, bitter houses of the unemployed, to "God's quartette": the widow, the orphan, the sick, the stranger at the gate.[68] To him, the life of lonely prayers and frugal study in the woods, stayed bereft of a God-given opportunity for blissfulness: Tzedakah. A tzaddik, he felt, is not merely a righteous man. To deserve that appellation one must give Tzedakah, charity, of what one has, of what one knows, of what one is.

In his "Iggeret ha-Kodesh"[69] (Letter of Holiness)

he expands his teaching: "Tzedakah is the greatest of all Mitzvot. Israel will be redeemed only through the practice of Tzedakah.[70] Did not Rabbi Shimeon proclaim that he who gives Tzedakah to the poor sanctifies God's name every day? The reward for sowing Tzedakah is the quality of truth. Remember: *"The work of Tzedakah shall be peace and the effect of Tzedakah quiet and confidence forever!"*[71]

When Isaiah described how *"He* (the Lord) *put Tzedakah as a coat of mail and as a helmet of salvation upon His head,"*[72] our Sages of blessed memory commented: Just as in a coat of mail, every small scale joins with the others to form one piece of armor, so does every perutah (penny) spent on charity combine with the rest to form a large sum.[73] Whilst the bases of the Jewish life are HaBaD (Hakhmah, Binah, Deah — wisdom, understanding, knowledge), there is no mitzvah more noble than Tzedakah: "Tzedakah fashions a garment of glory for the soul, emanating from the light of God and embracing all the worlds. A tzaddik first gives the coin to the poor and only then offers his prayer. *"Only through the act of charity do I see Thy face,*[74] for the grace of God looms over those who revere Him from everlasting to everlasting." *"Let Tzedakah well up as a mighty stream,*[75] for it is the spark of divinity in his own soul, stemming from the sublime Wisdom of heaven."

XI

It was the passionate servant of God, the ruthless denouncer of evil, the loving Jeremiah, who, thousands of years earlier, had offered the endorsement of both Maimonides and the Rav of Liady in a synthesis of *da'at* and *ahavah,* priceless in its simplicity:[76]

Did not thy father eat and drink, and do justice and righteousness?
Then it was well with him.
He judged the cause of the poor and needy;
Then it was well.
Is not this to know Me? saith the Lord.

NOTES

1. Paragr. 5.
2. Beresh. XVIII:28.
3. Shem. XXI:23.
4. J. H. Hertz, Pentateuch, p. 405.
5. Kuzari, I:4.
6. "Or Adonai."
7. Midrash Mishle *ad locum.*
8. See David Kaufmann, "Attributenlehre," IV:4c, VII:3.
9. Ber. 57b.
10. Deb. VI:5.
11. *Ibid.,* IV:39.
12. A. Jellinek, "Thos. Aquinas."
13. "Symposium" 201.
14. Shulh. Arukh, Eben ha-Ezer, XXV and also Seneca, Epistles IX:6 — for a polar attitude.
15. Ps. VIII:5.
16. "Ahabat Hessed," introduction.
17. Iliad XVIII:25.
18. Babli San. 7a, Yer. San. IV:13.
19. Baba M. 32b.
20. Ps. CXLV:9, Jonah IV:11.
21. See Da'at Eloh. in Otzar Yissrael and the corresp. article in Jewish Encyclopedia.
22. Vay. XIX:18 and 34.
23. Ber. IV:1.
24. Kidd. 48b, Baba B. 83b.
25. B. Baba 8b and comment *a. l.*
26. Ps. CXXXIX:2 where *"re'a"* means "thought," also Targ. Onkel. on Bam XVI:28.
27. "Emunot ve-Deot," Intro.
28. J. MacTaggart, "Plotinus" and Fritz Heineman, "Plotinus" *passim.*
29. "Symposium," *l. c.*
30. Aristotle, Physics, III:4.
31. Maximus of Tyre, Dissert. XV.
32. Intro. to his commentary *ad hoc.*
33. A. Adler, "Guiding Human Misfits."
34. "Les Dormes Immediates de la Conscience," 1888.
35. W. C. Greene, "Moira," Harv. Univ. Press, 276 ff.
36. Consult the index in A. J. Taylor's famed volume.

37. The various definitions are found in D. Runes' Dictionary of Philosophy.
38. Ketub. 8b.
39. "Liebe und Erkenntnis," 5f.
40. "Provincial Letters," III:12.
41. In S. R. Hirsch's ingenious commentary on Ber. XLII:27.
42. "Modern Man in Search of a Soul," also "The Integration of Personality."
43. S. D. Gupta, "Hindu Mysticism," III:f.
44. Ber. Ra. XII:14.
45. Throughout the Tanakh.
46. Baba M. 16b.
47. Berak. 20a, Pess. 53b.
48. Rabbi A. I. Kook's precious phrase.
49. Prov. X:25.
50. Hov. ha-Levavot, III.
50a. Isaiah V:16.
51. Israel Frankel, "Peshat," Toronto, 1956.
52. "Fallen Angels," Dropsie College, 1926.
53. His "Mitpahat Sefarim" versus his edition of the Siddur.
54. IX:6.
55. XII:7.
56. 3, 4, 6, 12.
57. Yer. Peah, I:1.
58. Yessode ha-Torah, I:1.
59. M. Teitelbaum, "ha-Rav mi-Liady" I.
60. Rambam on Prophecy, Kobetz, II.
61. The Alenu Prayer.
62. Shabbat 75a.
63. Isaiah V:12.
64. III:54.
65. Baba B. 10a.
66. Ibid., 9a.
67. Ibid.
68. Deb. XV and XVI.
69. See note 56.
70. Baba B. 9-10a.
71. Isaiah XXXII:17.
72. Ibid., LIX:17.
73. Baba B. I:c.
74. Ps. XVII:15.
75. Amos V:24.
76. Jer. XXII:15, 16.